Dolly Bureau
volume 1

Doll Patterns and Fashion
Megann R. Zabel

Copyright © 2013 by Megann R. Zabel
Published by MegannArt

All rights reserved. **Patterns are for personal use only and may not be used in any form for profit.** No part of this book may be reproduced in any form without the author's written permission except in the case of brief quotations in critical articles and reviews. For more information, contact the author of MegannArt at info@dollybureau.com or http://megannart.com.

The author is not affiliated with any doll company. The photos, patterns, and opinions expressed in this book do not reflect the opinions of any companies.

Refer to the "photo credits" section in the back of this book or the bottom of each photograph for doll manufacturer information.

ISBN-13: 978-0989384100
ISBN-10: 0989384101

Dedication:

Firstly, a big thanks Alison Rasmussen who helped guide me through the book publishing process in the doll world. Also, thank you for all your encouragement and support.

I would also like to extend a special thanks to all those doll companies who have given expressed permission to use their lovely dolls and doll-related items.

To Yvonne McCarty, my longtime friend and graphics instructor in high school. Thanks for helping me learn how to use graphics programs like a champ.

Also, thank you to all my family and friends who have encouraged me to do something this big, especially my mother and Steve.

Table of Contents:

Photos of Doll Designs	2-25
Doll Comparison Photos & Info	26-39
Understanding this Book	41
Sewing Pattern Basics	42-44
Closures	45-47
Fabric & Findings	48-49
Patterns	50-89
Photo Credits	90-91

Pattern on pages 78-79

Pattern on pages 62-63

Pattern on pages 56-58

Poppy Parker ©Integrity Toys, Inc. www.integritytoys.com

Poppy Parker ©Integrity Toys, Inc. www.integritytoys.com

Peppermint by Asleep Eidolon. All rights reserved. www.aedoll.cn

momoko™ ©PetWORKs Co., Ltd. Produced by SEKIGUCHI Co., Ltd. www.momokodoll.com

Pattern on pages 80-81

Pattern on pages 88-89

Fairy of Bugs Lady Bee & Punky Beetle
©Peak's Woods. All rights reserved.
www.peakswoods.net

Fairy of Bugs Lady Bee & Punky Beetle
©Peak's Woods. All rights reserved.
www.peakswoods.net

Pattern on page 87

Poppy Parker & Chip dolls ©Integrity Toys, Inc. www.integritytoys.com

momoko hoodie & dress on J-doll

momoko dress on Limhwa Mari

ToYou Mari 27 cm ball-jointed doll by Limhwa Dolls

Chip sweater on Ken

Fashionista Sporty Ken ©Mattel

Misaki outfit on Liv

momoko dress on Pullip

ToYou Mari 27 cm ball-jointed doll by Limhwa Dolls

momoko dress on Liv

Liv in Color! Sophie ©Spin Master, Ltd. www.spinmaster.com

Doll Comparison Sizes

The patterns in this book have been sized specifically for certain dolls; however, depending on the pattern, it may fit other dolls. Please see the list below for other dolls that may fit these patterns and fashion.

momoko: Blythe, Susie, Limhwa 27 cm tall ball-jointed dolls (such as Mari & Sara), J-doll, Pullip, Skipper, Azone Pure Neemo, Jenny, Liv.

Poppy Parker/Misaki: Dynamite Girls, Model Muse.

Chip: Ken.

1:4 scale ball-jointed dolls: Variety of "MSD" sized ball-jointed dolls, Ellowyne Wilde.

1:12 scale ball-jointed dolls: Variety of 16 cm sized ball-jointed dolls, Lati Yellow, Odeco&Nikki, Tiny Betsy McCall.

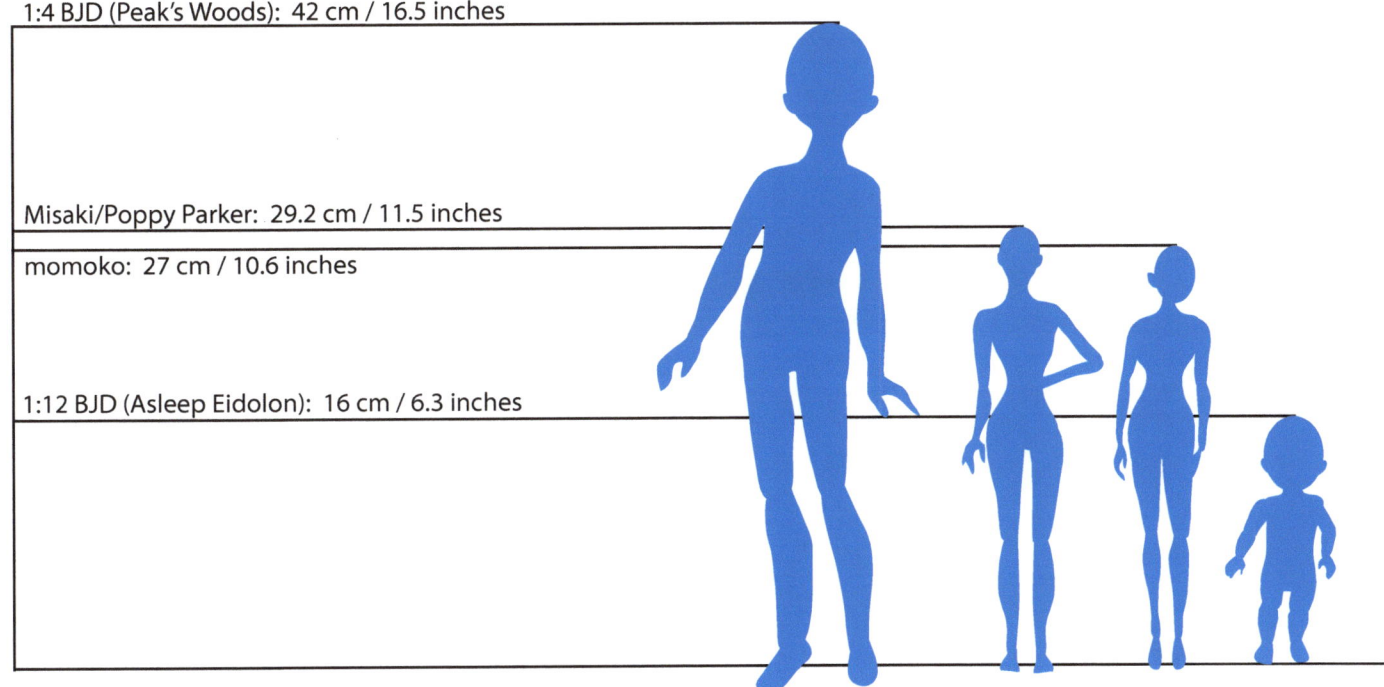

1:4 BJD (Peak's Woods): 42 cm / 16.5 inches

Misaki/Poppy Parker: 29.2 cm / 11.5 inches

momoko: 27 cm / 10.6 inches

1:12 BJD (Asleep Eidolon): 16 cm / 6.3 inches

Understanding this book:

Experience Level:
This pattern book is beginner to intermediate. Some basic sewing experience is recommended. Jewelry-making experience is helpful as well.

Reading Patterns:
Below are some basic guidelines in understanding the formatting and directions for patterns in this book.

1. All pattern pieces throughout the book will have a CAPITALIZED label, including in the directions.
2. Please see the box below for a legend of sewing symbols on patterns.
3. All patterns are meant for hook-and-loop, hook-and-eye, or bead-and-loop fasteners. See *Closures* section on pages 45-47.

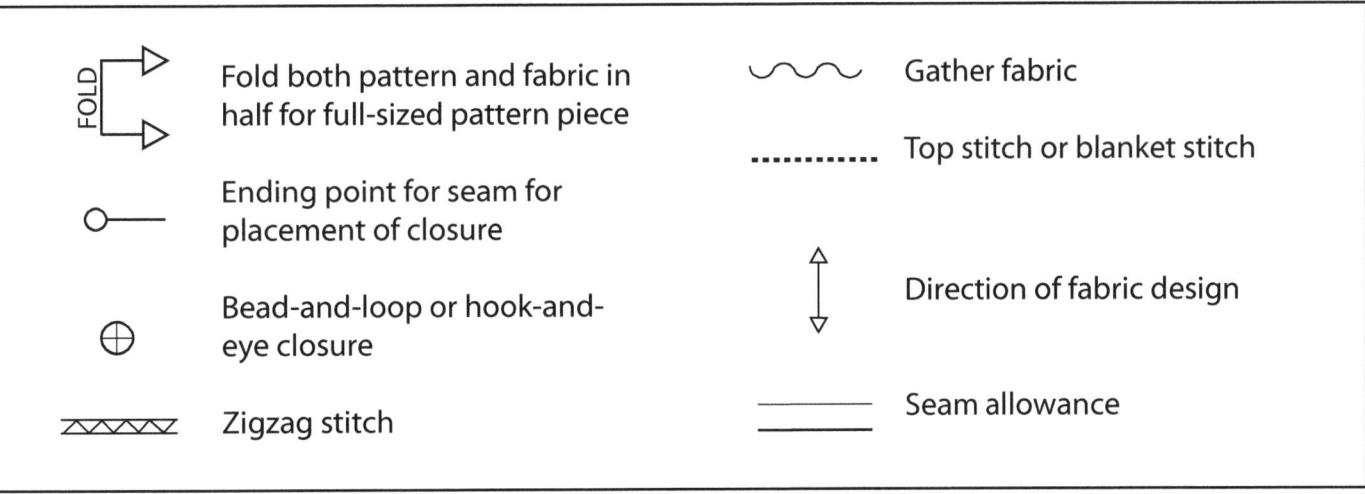

Tracing and Cutting Patterns:
To trace patterns without cutting up this book, trace all features of pattern using tissue paper. Cut out pattern pieces. Pin the tissue paper to desired fabric and cut out each piece before beginning the sewing directions.

Sewing Pattern Basics:

For each of the patterns in this book, the below items will be required. In the directions for each pattern, there will be a "sewing pattern basics" notation. Refer to the list below for pattern requirements.

1. **Tissue paper** and **pen** for tracing patterns. See *Tracing and Cutting Patterns* on page 41.
2. **Fabric** to fit pattern pieces. Every pattern in this book requires less than 1 yard of fabric, unless otherwise specified in pattern directions.
3. **Sewing machine** with appropriate **threads** for garment.
4. **Sewing pins**.
5. **Scissors**.
6. **Iron**. Pressing edges makes a garment look finished and clean. However, some fabrics may not be iron-friendly.

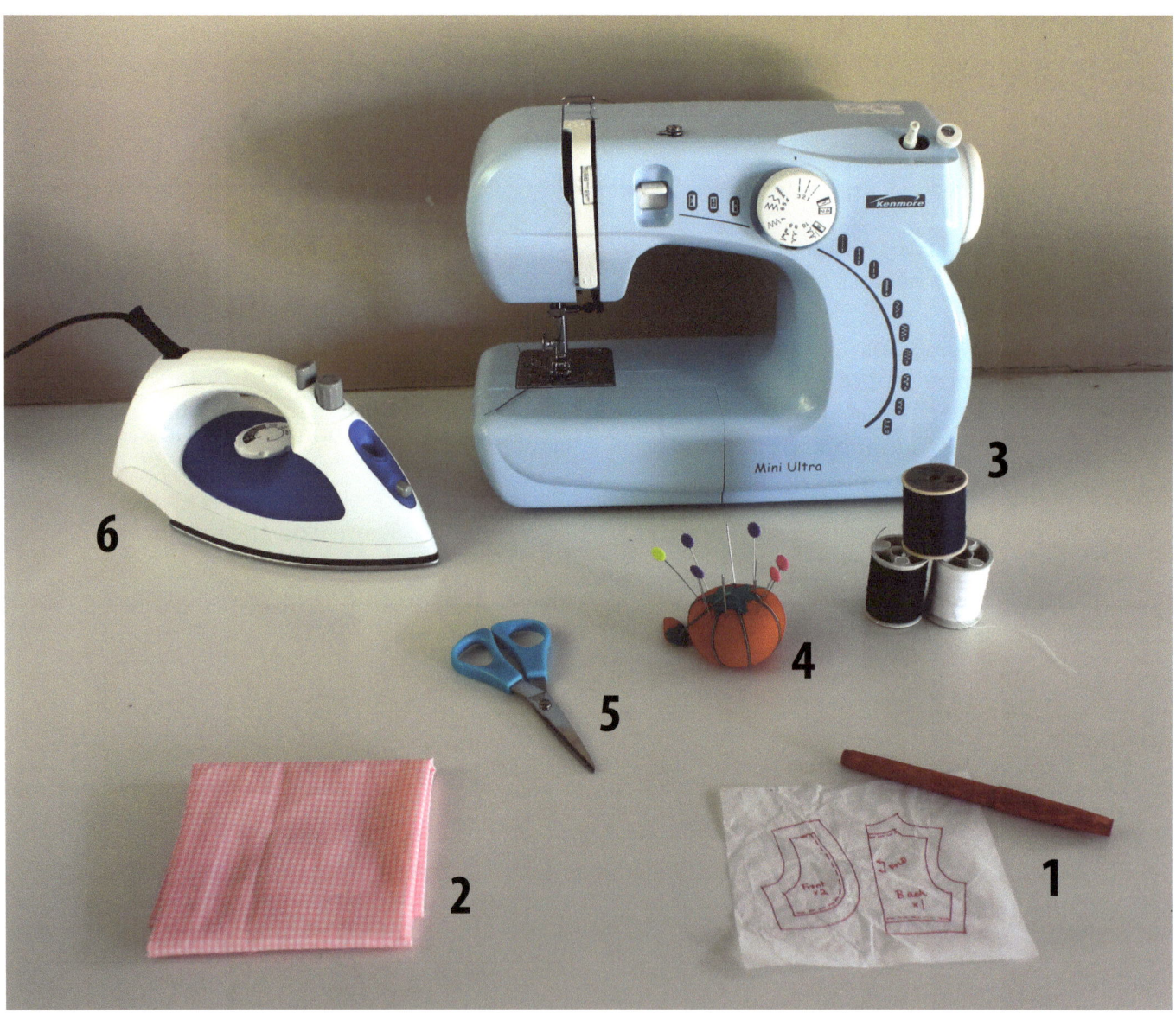

Optional Sewing Items:

Some of the items below are helpful and recommended, although not necessarily required.

1. **Hemostats**. Turning inside out those tiny sleeves can be difficult. Using hemostats makes it much easier.
2. **Seam ripper**. Pull out threads easily with this tool.
3. **Measuring tape**. This can be helpful if resizing or double checking lengths of pattern pieces. Some patterns require cutting a certain length of ribbon or lace, which may need to be measured. See the back of this book for a basic ruler.
4. **Corner turner**. Sewing machines can sometimes have a hard time sewing corners. Using this tool when feeding fabric through a sewing machine may help.
5. **Rotary cutter.** This tool will help cut larger pieces of fabric quickly. The cutting mat used with a rotary cutting tool is not pictured.
6. **Anti-fray adhesive** (not pictured). Some of those edges in fabric will try to fray even though they are on the inside of the garment. Using an anti-fray adhesive like Dritz Fray Check can help reduce fraying.

Note: Other items may be required for patterns. Please see individual pattern "supplies" lists for further information.

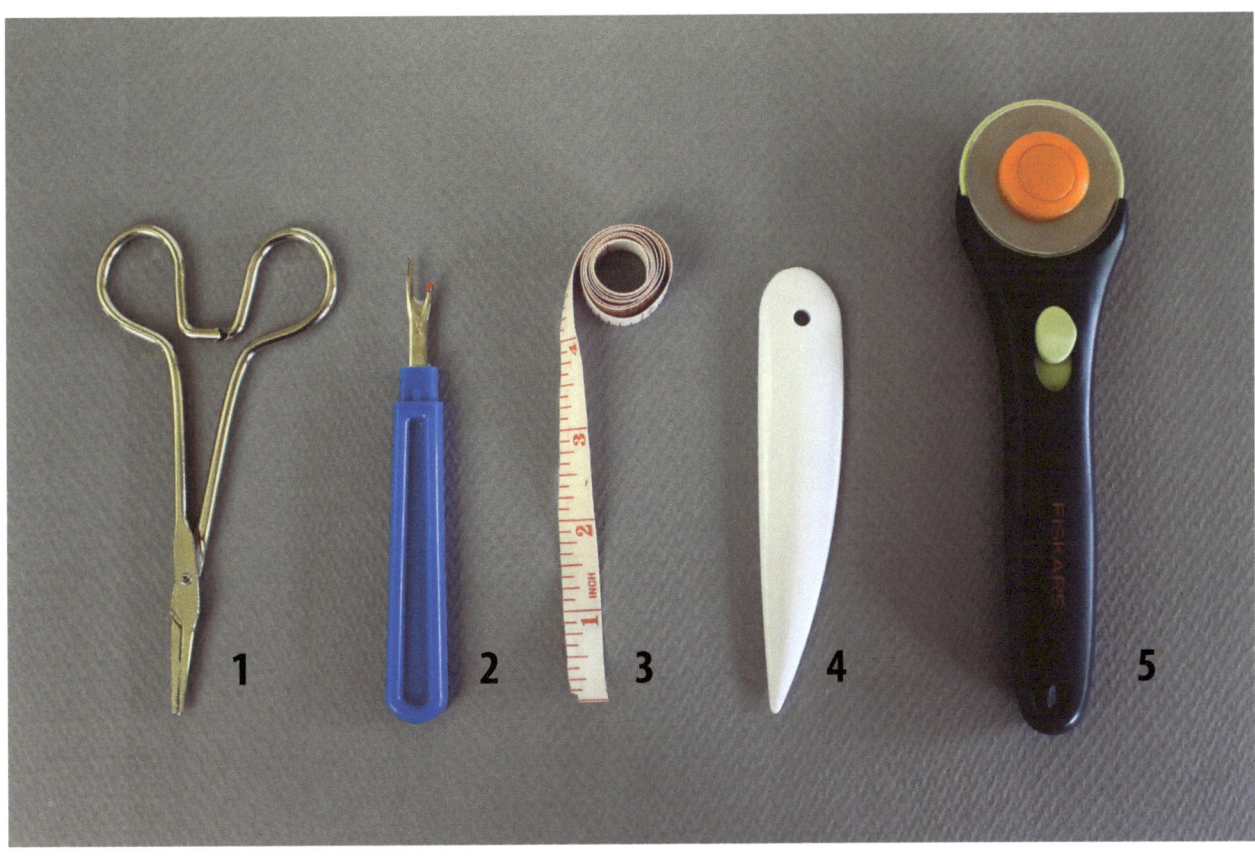

Sewing Terminology Defined:

Basting stitch: Loosely applying a temporary sewing stitch to hold layers of fabric in place. This method can be helpful if trying to *ease* fabric.

Blanket stitch: A type of interlocking stitch often used on unhemmed fabric.

Ease: Bring fabrics together to fit an area without causing any puckers. Sewing pins are helpful for this task as well as using a basting stitch method. See *basting stitch*.

Gather: Shortening the length of fabric so that the gathered (longer) piece of fabric can be attached to a shorter piece.

Pleat: Folding cloth by doubling textile on itself, typically finished by pressing and/or stitching the folds into place.

Ruffle: Gathered or goffered lace or other cloth textile used ornamentally on a garment.

Top stitch: Stitching close to the edge or seam on the top or right side of the garment.

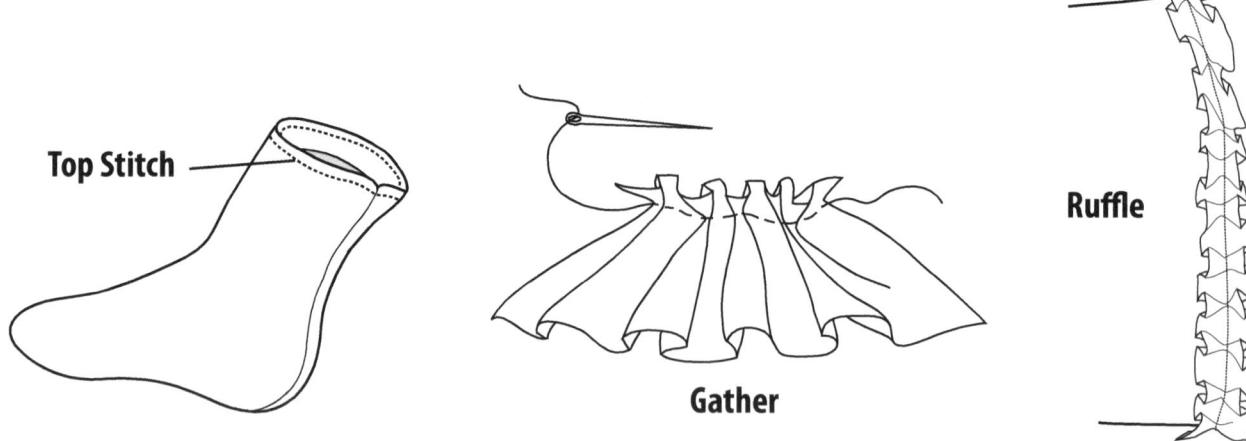

Closures:

All patterns in this book are meant for bead-and-loop, hook-and-eye, or hook-and-loop fasteners. Please see the diagram below for closure materials used on the patterns in this book.

1. **Bead-and-loop closure.** Very affordable method of using crocheting twine tied into a loop and a bead.
2. **Hook-and-eye closure.** This is an alternative to the bead-and-loop closure, but uses the same directions for seams and top stitching.
3. **Hook-and-loop closure.** Commonly known as Velcro. This is more helpful when longer closures are needed.
4. **Snaps.** The patterns in this book **do not** have allowances for fabric to overlap for fasteners like snaps. If snaps are desired, take out pattern a bit to accommodate snaps.

See the following pages for directions on using closures.

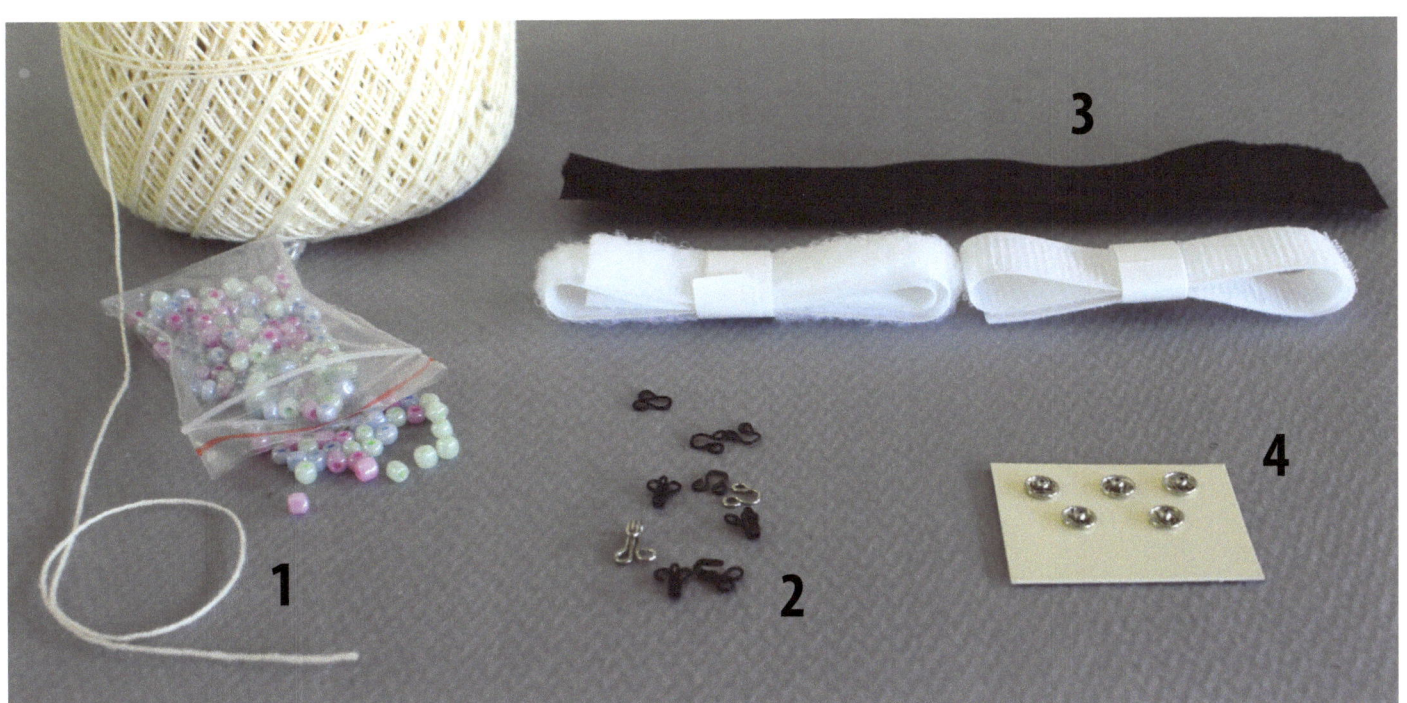

Closure Directions:

Refer to this page and the following for appropriate closure directions on selected doll garments.

Bead-and-loop (Figure A): Fold over remaining raw edges and top stitch, starting from the top part of one side of the opening, down to the seam, over the seam, and up to the end of the folded edges. Hand sew a bead-and-loop closure where indicated.

Hook-and-eye closures (Figure A): Use same directions as above, replacing the type of closure with a hook-and-eye.

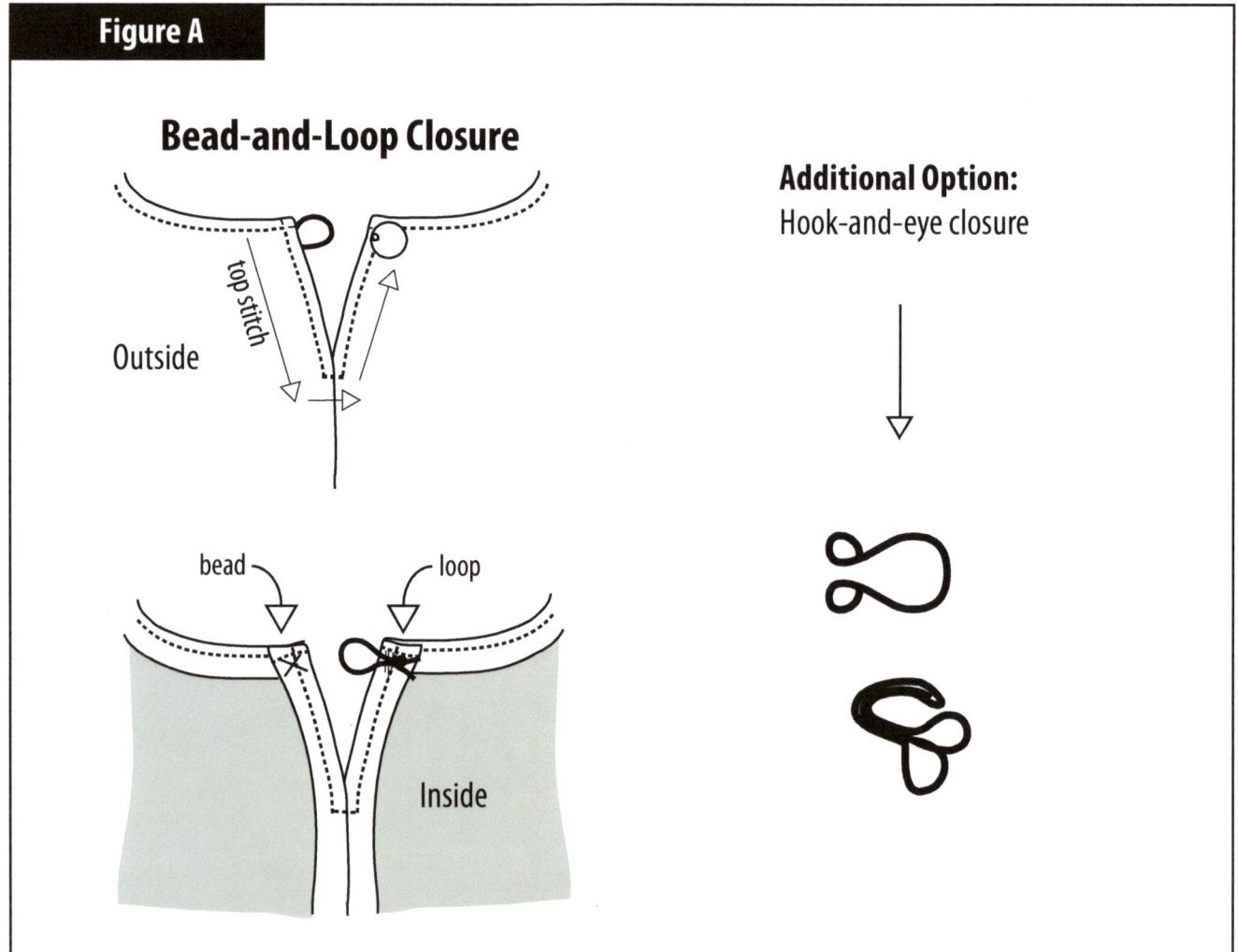

46

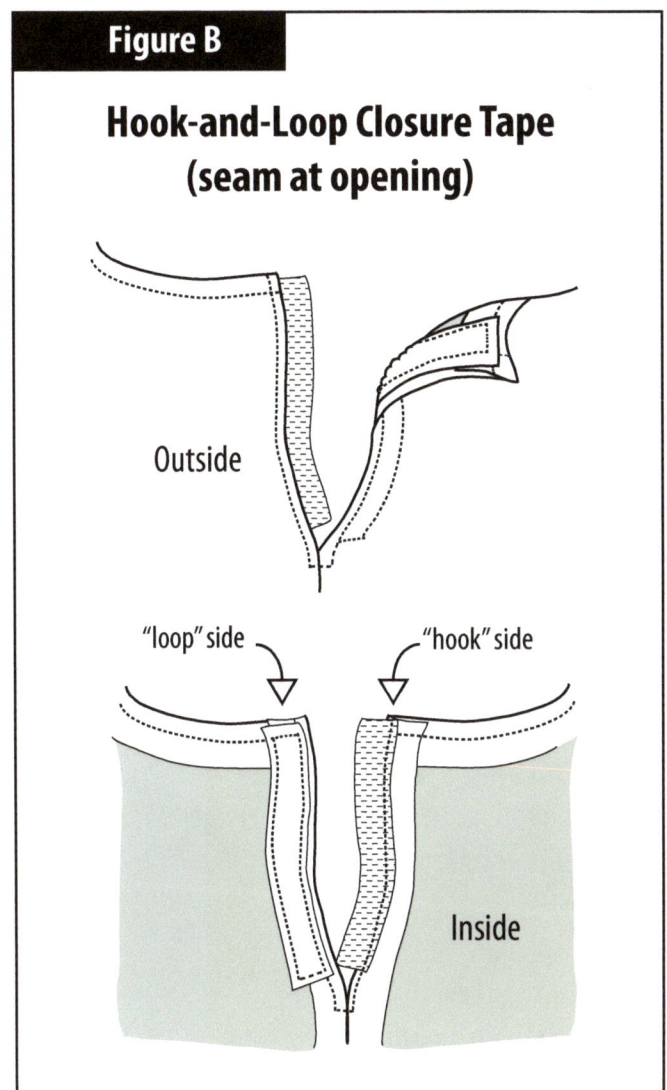

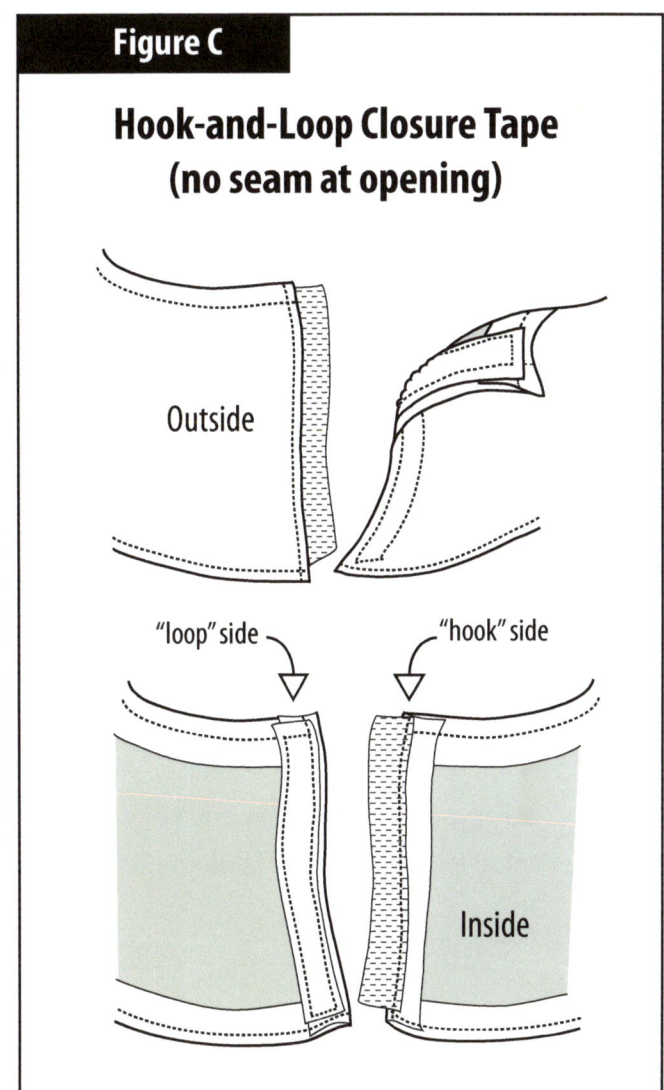

Hook-and-loop closures:

Seam at opening (Figure B): Fold over remaining raw edges. Place the "hook" side of the hook-and-loop tape just on the inside enough to top stitch. Make sure the hooked part of the closure is facing out. Top stitch over the closure, starting from the top part of one side of the opening, down to the seam, over the seam, and up to the end of the folded edges. Place the whole looped side of the hook-and-loop tape on the inside of the garment and top stitch in a rectangle.

No seam at opening (Figure C): Fold over remaining raw edges. Place the "hook" side of the hook-and-loop tape just on the inside enough to top stitch. Make sure the hooked part of the closure is facing out. Top stitch tape to garment. Place the whole looped side of the hook-and-loop tape on the inside of the garment and top stitch in a rectangle.

Fabric and Findings:

Acquiring the right fabrics and findings for doll clothing and fashions can be a challenge. See below for some recommendations on discovering the right items for your dolly project.

Fabric:

Density: Lightweight fabrics can be very important when sewing doll clothing since heavier fabrics will make seams and top stitching look bulky. To see if a fabric is lightweight enough, fold over the edge a couple of times and see if the width of fold appears too big.

Print: The size of prints, especially for 1:6 scale dolls and smaller, is important for a realistic looking garment. Aim for prints that are tiny.

Fray: Not interested in using a serger or anti-fray adhesive for those pesky unraveling edges of fabric? Try to look for fabrics with edges that will not fray quite as much.

Findings:

Seed Beads: Seed beads make great decorative accents on clothing, tiny buttons for small dolls, and jewelry. Pictured on the next page are a couple different sizes of white seed beads.

Lace and Fabric Applique: Tiny little lace and applique provides more interesting design for doll attire. Ribbon flowers, pictured on the next page, are often easy to find at a local craft store.

Buttons: With buttons, definitely the tinier the better. Pictured on the next page are 4 mm white buttons. 1:6 scale dolls and smaller often require at least this small of a button to look realistic. Also, using seed beads as tiny buttons will work.

Eyelets and Iron-On Metal Applique: Finding tiny versions of these add a finishing touch to doll clothing. Sometimes looking in the scrapbooking aisle of craft stores can turn up small versions of these items appropriate for dolls.

Jewelry Chain: Using a very fine jewelry chain will make doll jewelry appear more realistic. Also, keeping an eye out for small charms can make a perfect pendant on doll necklaces.

Remember, tiny, tiny, tiny!

momoko Hoodie Tutorial

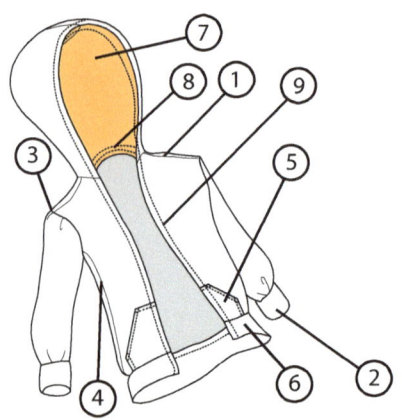

Follow the diagram above with the corresponding numbers and photographs throughout the tutorial.

Pattern Pieces:
FRONT x2, BACK x1, SLEEVE x2, CUFF x2, WAISTBAND x1, POCKET x2, and HOOD x2 for outside and lining ⇨

Supplies:
Sewing pattern basics (See pages 42-43)

Steps:
Before following the steps outlined in the diagram, cut enough of each pattern piece for this hoodie.

1. Sew shoulder seams of FRONT to BACK with the right sides together.

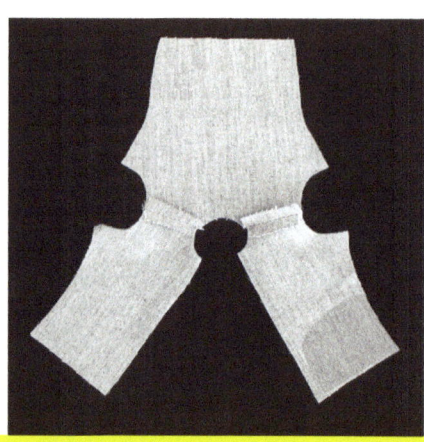

Press seams open.

2. Fold CUFF the long way with right sides showing. Make small gather where indicated on bottom of SLEEVE. With right sides together, sew seams of CUFF to bottom of SLEEVE.

Press SLEEVE/CUFF seams open.

3. Gather upper SLEEVE where indicated. Ease upper SLEEVE into each armhole using sewing pins or basting stitch.

With right sides together, sew seam and repeat for other SLEEVE.

Hoodie Tutorial

momoko

4. Sew seam from bottom of SLEEVE to armpit and then to the bottom of the garment. Repeat on other side.

Turn inside out.

5. For POCKET, fold over indicated edge in above picture. This will be the opening for each pocket on the hoodie. Top stitch this edge.

Fold over edges on either side of previously made top stitch. Place POCKET on hoodie and top stitch both parts onto the hoodie.

6. Make a gather on the bottom of BACK piece until hoodie bottom is same length as the WAISTBAND. Fold WAISTBAND in half the long way with right side exposed. With right sides together, sew seam of WAISTBAND to hoodie bottom using pins or basting stitch.

7. With right sides together, sew seam along curved side of outside HOOD pieces. Repeat for lining HOOD pieces. Clip curves.

With right sides together, sew seam of HOOD lining to outside pieces along front side of hood.

Turn hood inside out and top stitch along opening of hood.

Optional: Turn raw edge inside the hood and press. This will leave a clean edge inside the garment.

Hoodie Tutorial

8. With back side of hood (outside fabric) to right side of neck opening of hoodie, sew a seam. Make sure hood is in center of neck opening.

9. Fold over remaining raw edge of hoodie and top stitch from bottom of opening of hoodie up to hood, around neck opening, and down to other side of hoodie opening.

Done!

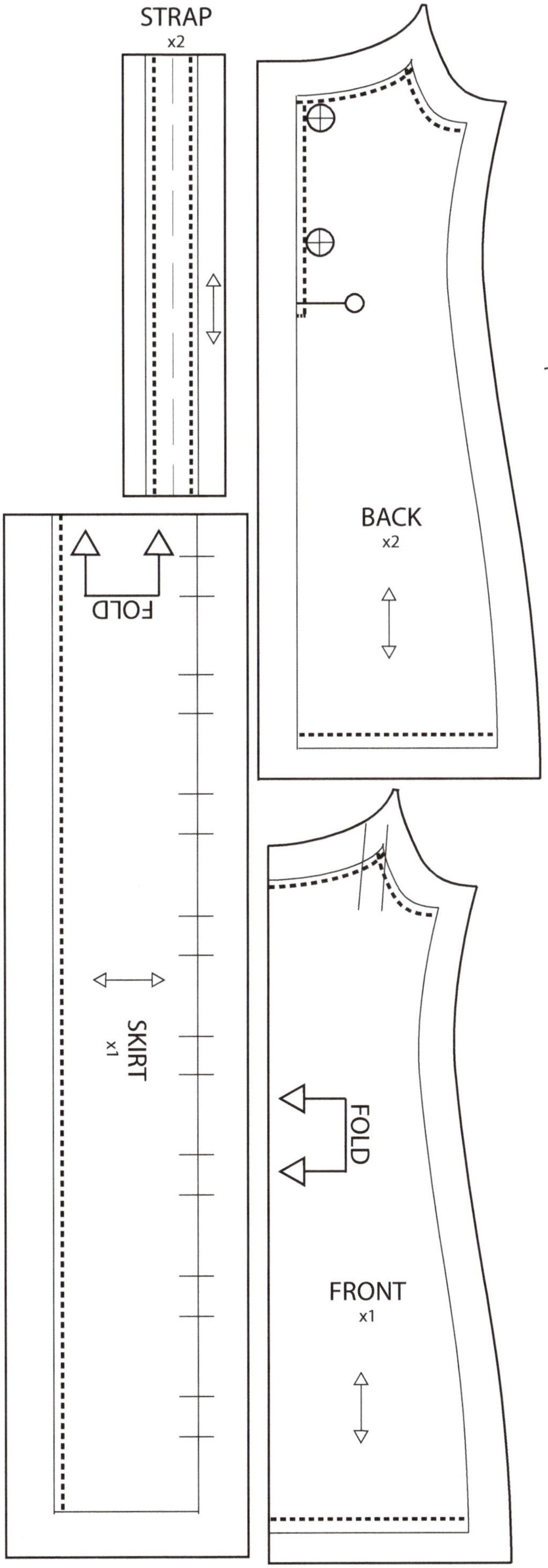

momoko

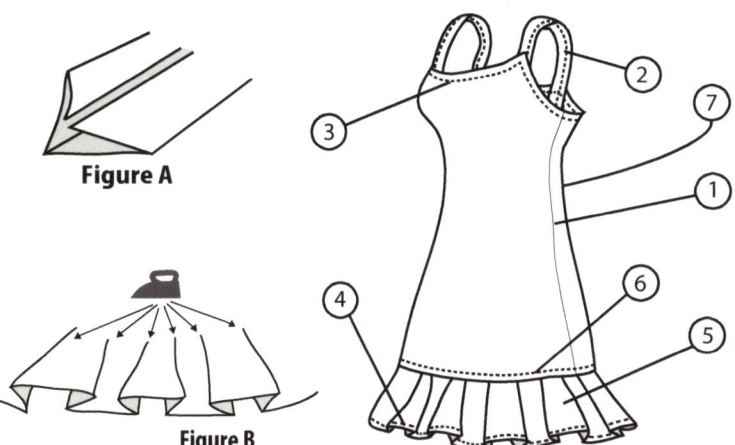

Figure A

Figure B

momoko
Pattern x100%

Dress:

Photos on pages 6-7.

Pattern Pieces:
FRONT x1, BACK x2, SKIRT x1, and STRAP x2

Supplies:
Sewing pattern basics (See pages 26-27)
Bead-and-loop closure

Steps:
Before following the steps outlined in the diagram, cut enough of each pattern piece for this dress.

1. With right sides together, sew seam down side of FRONT to a BACK piece. Repeat with other BACK piece. Press seams.
2. Fold STRAP in half and press with iron. Fold each of those halves inward (see Figure A) and press. Top stitch folded STRAP. Repeat with other STRAP.
3. Fold over top seam of FRONT and BACK pieces. Pin straps in place where indicated on pattern. Check strap placement and length on doll. Top stitch over FRONT and BACK pieces as well as straps.
4. Fold over bottom of SKIRT and top stitch.
5. Fold skirt over at markings indicated on SKIRT pattern. Press with iron to make box pleats (see Figure B).
6. With right sides together, sew seam of bottom of dress to SKIRT piece. Fold seam of SKIRT and dress seam up and top stitch along the dress (not skirt) side of garment.
7. With right sides together, sew seam from bottom of back of SKIRT piece up to ⎯○ point on pattern. Turn inside out. See pages 45-47 for a bead-and-loop *Closures* guide.

Misaki & Poppy Parker

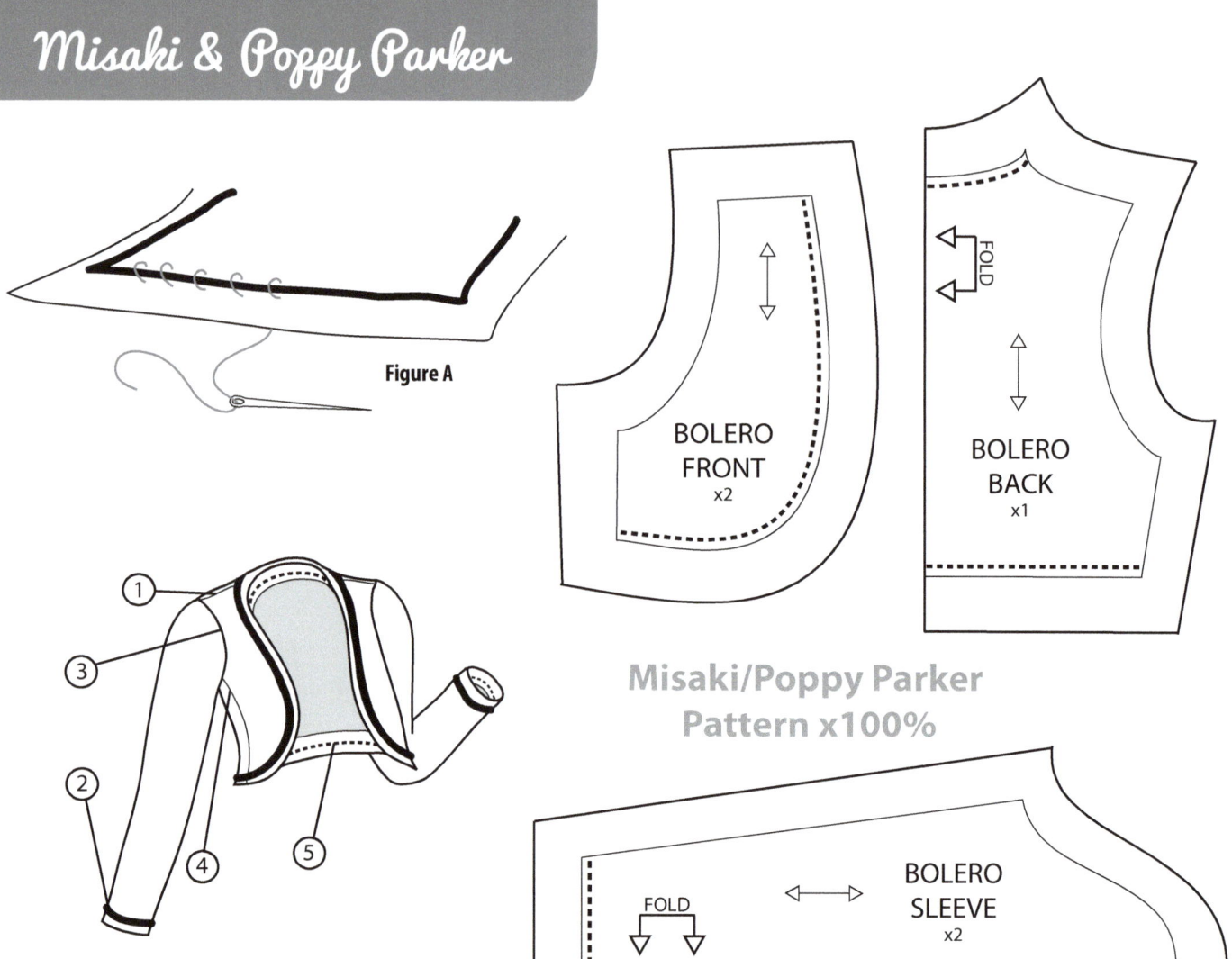

Figure A

Misaki/Poppy Parker Pattern x100%

Bolero:

Photo on page 10.

Pattern Pieces:
BOLERO FRONT x2, BOLERO BACK x1, and BOLERO SLEEVE x2

Supplies:
Sewing pattern basics (See pages 42-43)
Needle and thread
Twine for trim accent

Steps:
Before following the steps outlined in the diagram, cut enough of each pattern piece for this bolero.

1. Sew shoulder seams of BOLERO FRONT pieces to BOLERO BACK with the right sides together. Press seams open.
2. Fold bottom side of the BOLERO SLEEVE over and top stitch. Cut enough twine for the width of each sleeve opening. Attach twine with needle and thread (Figure A) directly over top stitch. Repeat for other BOLERO SLEEVE.
3. Ease upper BOLERO SLEEVE into each armhole using sewing pins or basting stitch. Make sure right sides are together. Sew seam and repeat for other BOLERO SLEEVE.
4. Sew seam from bottom of BOLERO SLEEVE to armpit and then to the bottom of the garment. Clip curves, especially at armpit area. Repeat on other side.
5. Fold over remaining open edge of bolero and top stitch. Attach twine with needle and thread directly over top stitch (Figure A).

Misaki & Poppy Parker

Skirt:

Photos on pages 10-11.

Pattern Pieces:
SKIRT FRONT x1, SKIRT SIDE x2, SKIRT BACK x2, and SKIRT FACING x1

Supplies:
Sewing pattern basics (See pages 42-43)
Needle and thread
Bead-and-loop closure
Twine for trim accent

Steps:
Before following the steps outlined in the diagram, cut enough of each pattern piece for this skirt.

1. Sew seam down SKIRT FRONT piece and SKIRT SIDE piece marked "front" with right sides together. Repeat with other SKIRT SIDE piece and other side of SKIRT FRONT. NOTE: On one side only, sew from the top of the garment down to the dash mark on the pattern for the slit. Press seams open.
2. Sew seam down "front" SKIRT BACK piece and SKIRT SIDE piece with right sides together. Repeat with other SKIRT BACK and SKIRT FRONT pieces. Press seams open.
3. Fold over bottom of SKIRT FACING and top stitch. Using pins or a basting stitch may be helpful for this step.
4. With right sides together, sew seam of top of skirt to top of SKIRT FACING. Turn inside out and top stitch waistline of garment.
5. Fold over bottom of skirt and slit. Top stitch. Attach twine with needle and thread (Figure A) directly over top stitch.
6. With right sides together, sew seam from bottom of skirt to ⎯⎯○ point on pattern. Turn inside out. See pages 45-47 for a bead-and-loop *Closures* guide.

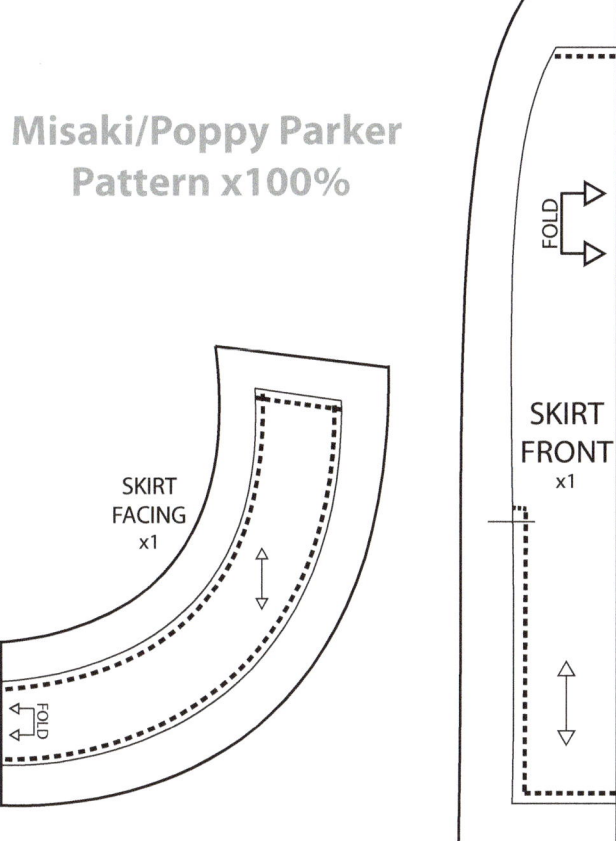

Misaki/Poppy Parker Pattern x100%

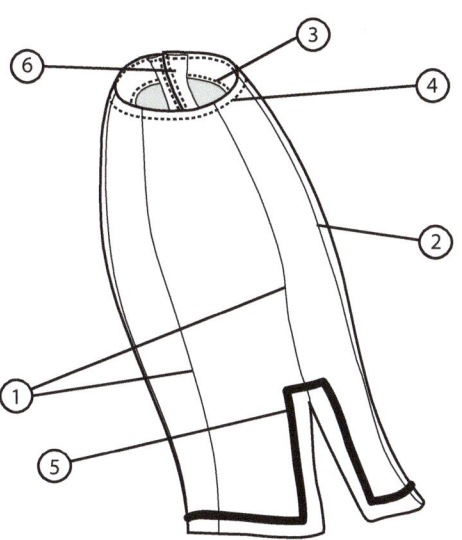

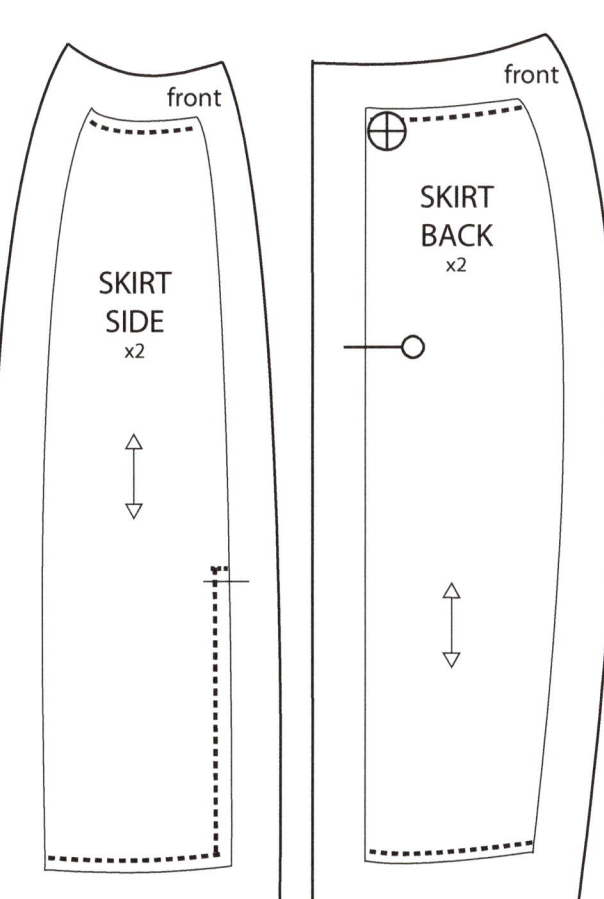

57

Misaki & Poppy Parker

Figure B

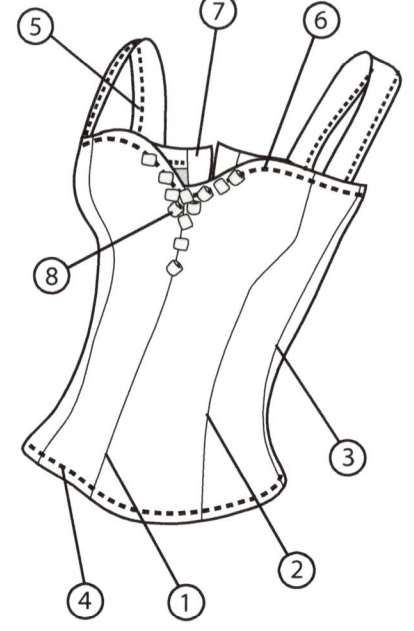

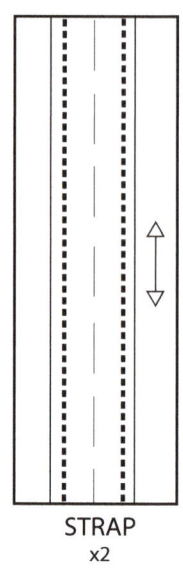

STRAP
x2

Top:

Photos on pages 10-11.

Pattern Pieces:
FRONT x2, SIDE x2, BACK x2, FACING x1, and STRAP x2

Supplies:
Sewing pattern basics (See pages 42-43)
Needle and thread
Hook-and-loop closure tape
Seed beads

Steps:
Before following the steps outlined in the diagram, cut enough of each pattern piece for this top.

1. Sew seam down FRONT pieces marked "front" with right sides together. Press seams open.

2. Sew seam down FRONT piece and SIDE piece marked "front" with right sides together. Repeat with other FRONT and SIDE pieces. Press seams open.

3. Sew seam down SIDE piece and BACK piece marked "front" with right sides together. Repeat with other SIDE and BACK pieces. Press seams open.

4. Fold bottom side of garment over and top stitch.

5. Fold STRAP in half and press with iron. Fold each of those halves inward (Figure B) and press. Top stitch folded STRAP. Repeat with other STRAP.

6. Fold over bottom of FACING and top stitch. With right sides together, sew seam of top of garment to top of FACING. Turn inside out and pin straps to inside of garment where specified on pattern. Top stitch garment, facing, and straps.

7. Fold over open edge of back pieces and sew hook and loop fastener into back of garment. See pages 45-47 for a helpful hook-and-loop *Closures* guide.

8. Hand sew seed beads on front side of top.

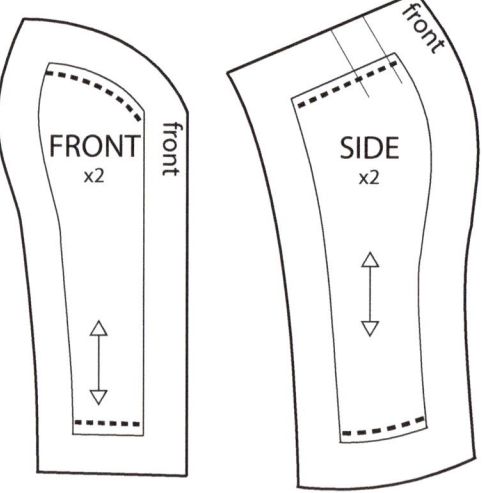

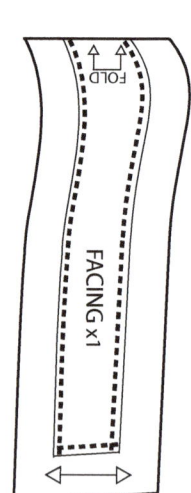

Misaki/Poppy Parker Pattern x100%

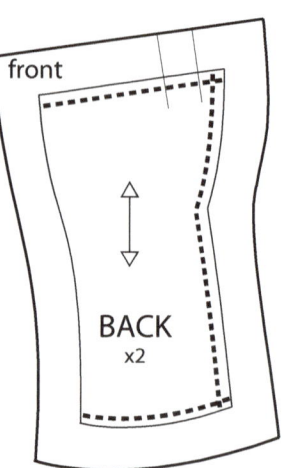

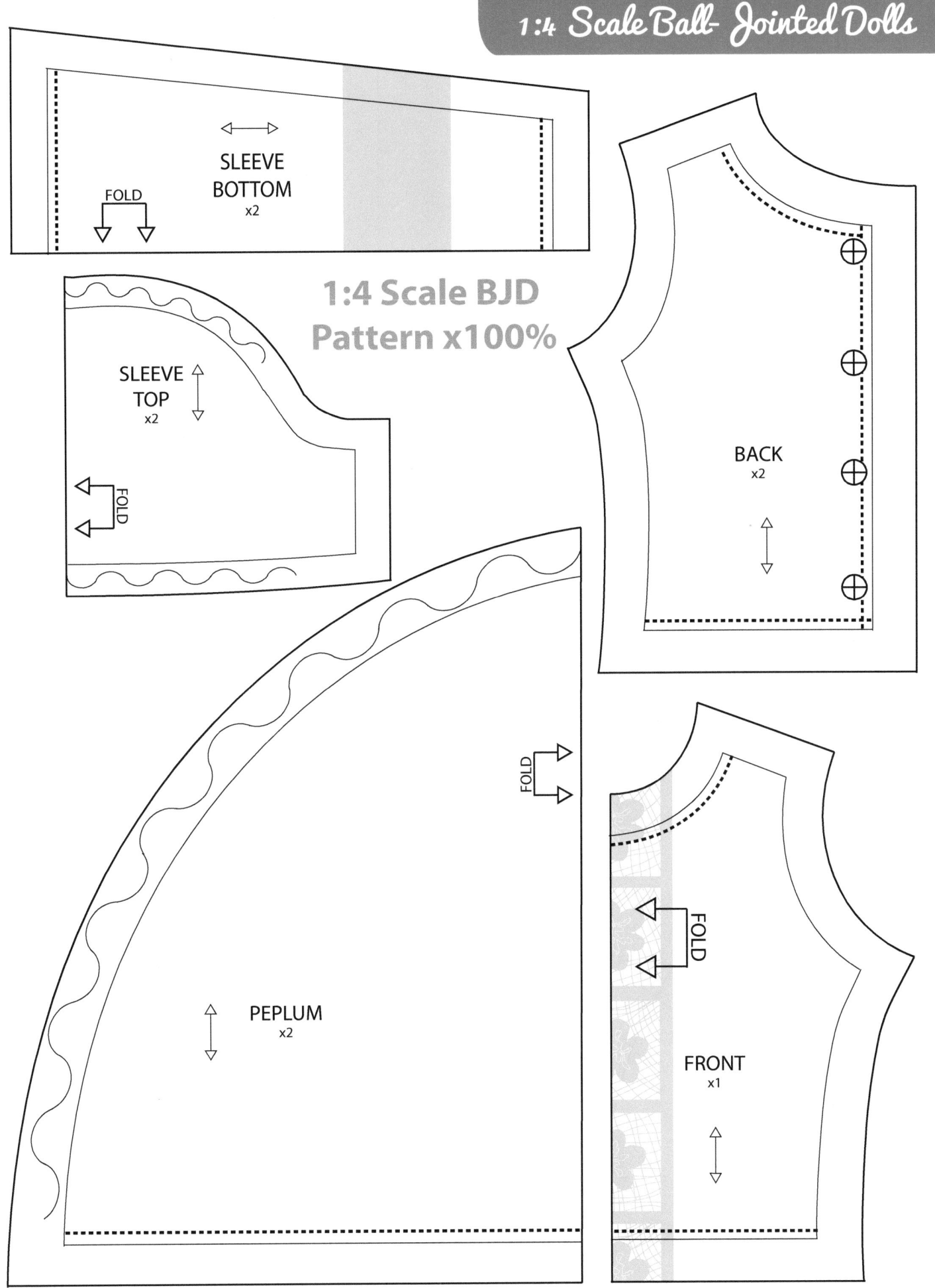

1:4 Scale Ball-Jointed Dolls

Underskirt:

Photos on pages 8-9.

Pattern Pieces:
SKIRT x1 and BELT x1

Supplies:
Sewing pattern basics (See pages 42-43)
Bead-and-loop closure
Needle and thread

Steps:
Before following the steps outlined in the diagram, cut enough of each pattern piece for this underskirt. Note: Pattern needs to be extended to full size. Tulle is recommended for the SKIRT and will help make the dress skirt more full. As a result of using tulle, a hem is not provided for the bottom of this pattern. Basic cotton is recommended for the BELT of the underskirt.

Skirt is meant for a doll with waist to feet length of approximately 9 inches and waist circumference of approximately 7-1/2 inches. Add or subtract appropriate amount of to pattern, if necessary.

1. On the SKIRT, gather where indicated until gather is the length of the BELT. With right sides together, pin gathered fabric every 1/2 inch to inch to the BELT. Sew seam.
2. Fold BELT over seam and top stitch the top and bottom of belt (Figure A).
3. With right sides together, sew seam from bottom of back of SKIRT up to ─○ point on pattern. Turn inside out. See pages 45-47 for a bead-and-loop *Closures* guide.

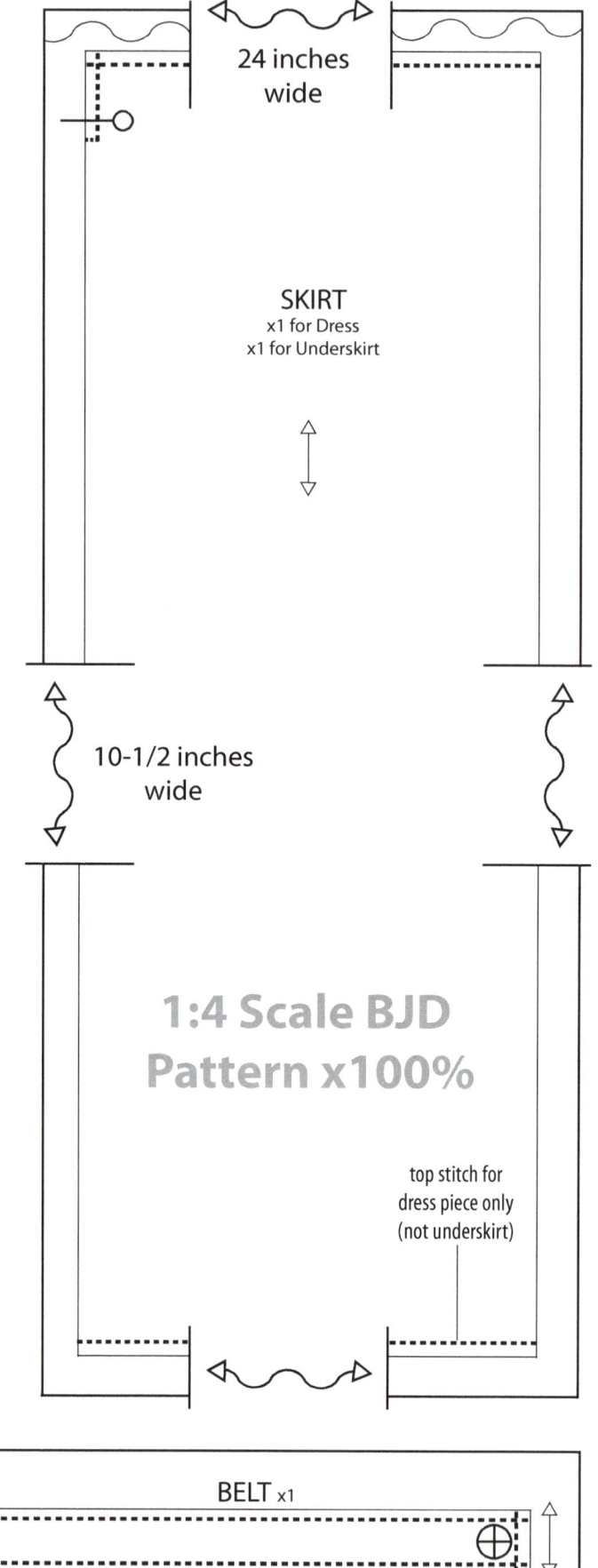

SKIRT
x1 for Dress
x1 for Underskirt

24 inches wide

10-1/2 inches wide

1:4 Scale BJD Pattern x100%

top stitch for dress piece only (not underskirt)

BELT x1

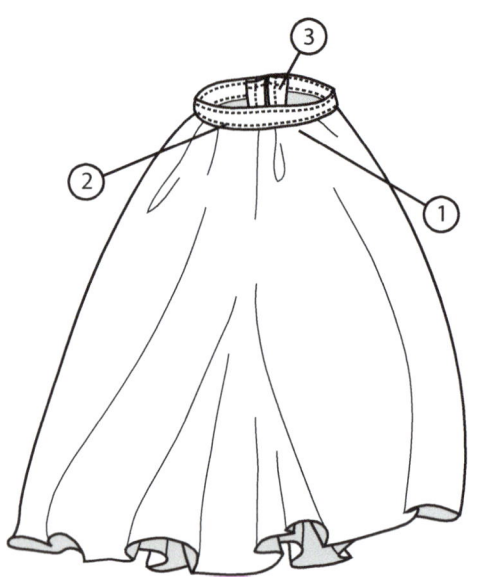

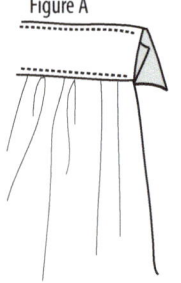

Figure A

Hat:

Photos on pages 8-9.

Supplies:
Glue gun
Needle and Thread
Straw hat
Ribbon
Button
Beads

Steps:

1. Cut enough ribbon to cover the circumference of the brim. Hot glue ends of ribbon where flower is planned to be placed.
2. Cut another small piece of ribbon. Make sure ends of ribbon are cut at about a 45 degree angle. Fold ribbon in half and with flower on top, hot glue to hat.
3. Right on top of the flower, sew button directly onto hat.
4. Sew beads on one side of the flower, directly onto the hat and brim ribbon. Repeat for other side of flower.

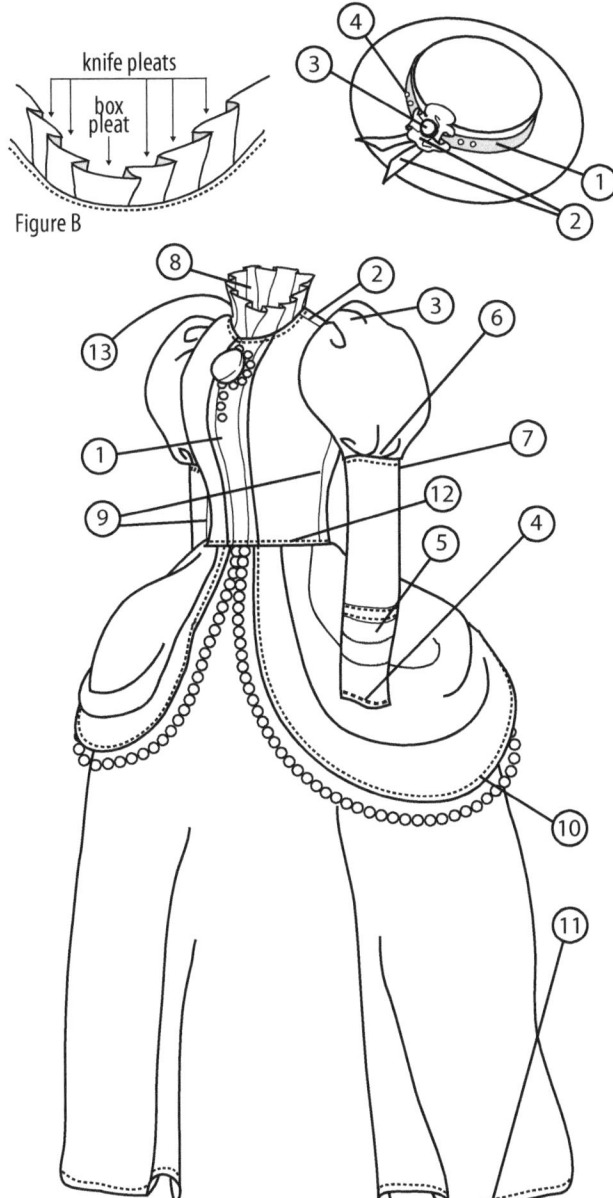

1:4 Scale Ball- Jointed Dolls

Dress:

Photos on pages 8-9.

Pattern Pieces:
FRONT x1, BACK x2, SLEEVE TOP x2, SLEEVE BOTTOM x2, PEPLUM x2, and SKIRT x1 (pattern on pages 59-60)

Supplies:
Sewing pattern basics (See pages 42-43)
Needle and thread
Hook-and-loop closure tape
Beads
Ribbon with beaded edges
Lace and ribbon
Button

Steps:
Before following the steps outlined in the diagram, cut enough of each pattern piece for this dress. A satin-like fabric was used for the dress and velveteen was used for the peplums.

1. Sew desired lace and ribbon vertically over the front of the FRONT piece.
2. Sew shoulder seams of FRONT to BACK with the right sides together. Press seams open.
3. Gather upper SLEEVE TOP where indicated, trying to match the length of the gather to the FRONT and BACK armhole length. Ease upper SLEEVE TOP into each armhole using sewing pins or basting stitch. Make sure right sides are together. Sew seam and repeat for other SLEEVE TOP.
4. Fold bottom side of each SLEEVE BOTTOM over and top stitch.
5. In gray shaded area on each SLEEVE BOTTOM, sew desired lace and ribbon.
6. Gather each lower SLEEVE TOP where indicated until gather is the length of the upper portion of the SLEEVE BOTTOM. With right sides together, sew seam of SLEEVE TOP gather to upper SLEEVE BOTTOM.
7. Top stitch upper portion of each SLEEVE BOTTOM.
8. Cut approximately 13 inches of 5/8 inch wide ribbon. With right sides together at the middle of the top of the FRONT pattern piece, pin one ribbon box pleat in place (see Figure B). Flaring out from the box pleat, pin knife pleats in place all the way around the FRONT and BACK neck opening. Sew seam. Fold over garment neck opening and top stitch along neckline. If ribbon is iron-friendly, press ribbon and seam.
9. With right sides together, sew seam from bottom of one armhole opening up to the armpit then down to join the FRONT and BACK pieces. Clip curves, particularly around armpit area. Repeat with other side. Turn sleeves inside out.
10. Cut enough of ribbon with beaded edge for the length of the straight edge of each PEPLUM. Fold straight edge of each PEPLUM over and top stitch with ribbon pinned to the back of the fabric. Ribbon should be held in place with top stitch.
11. Fold bottom side of SKIRT over and top stitch.
12. Make large gathers of curved part of each PEPLUM, making length of gather approximately 3-1/4 inches. With right sides together, pin gathered PEPLUM to the middle of bottom of FRONT piece, around to the BACK piece. Repeat with other PEPLUM over to other side of garment. Sew seam. On the SKIRT, gather where indicated until gather is the length of the bottom of the BACK and FRONT pieces. With right side of SKIRT facing back side of each PEPLUM, pin gathered SKIRT fabric every 1/2 inch to 1 inch. Sew seam over previously made seam. Fold seam of both PEPLUM pieces and SKIRT up and top stitch along the FRONT and BACK pieces of garment.
13. With right sides together, sew seam from bottom of back of SKIRT up to o—— point on pattern. Turn inside out. See pages 45-47 for a hook-and-loop tape *Closures* guide.

61

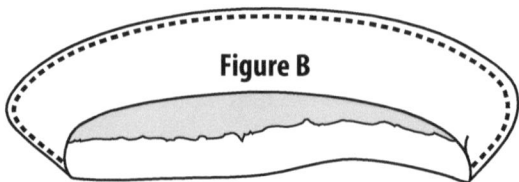

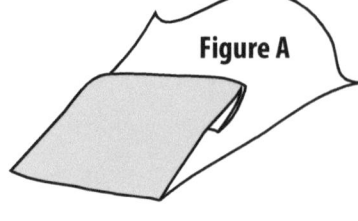

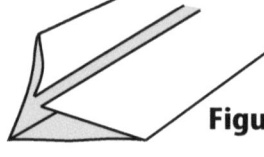

Coat:

Photo on page 5.

Pattern Pieces:
FRONT x2, BACK x1, SLEEVE x2, BELT x1, and COLLAR x2

Supplies:
Sewing pattern basics (See pages 42-43)
Buttons, rivets, or iron-on metal appliqué
Buckle
Crochet cotton thread or braided sewing thread
Sewing needle with large eye (darning needle)

Steps:
Before following the steps outlined in the diagram, cut enough of each pattern piece for this coat. This pattern works best with a fabric backside that is pleasing to the eye, since the backside of the fabric will be used as the sleeve cuff.

1. Sew shoulder seams of FRONT to BACK with the right sides together. Press seams open.
2. Fold bottom of SLEEVE over, exposing the back side, and top stitch. This seam is the opposite of a normal seam. Reveal the back side of the fabric (see part of Figure A). Repeat for other SLEEVE.
3. Gather upper SLEEVE where indicated. Ease upper SLEEVE into each armhole using sewing pins. Make sure right sides are together. Sew seam and repeat for other SLEEVE.
4. With right sides together, sew seam around outer curve of COLLAR. Make sure to leave open area to turn inside out. Clip curves as pictured on collar pattern. Turn inside out.
5. If possible, turn open end of COLLAR inside and press (Figure B). This will leave a clean edge in the coat, although is optional. Top stitch seam of COLLAR.
6. With the underside of the COLLAR facing the right side of the BACK and FRONT pieces, ease the pieces using pins or basting stitch. The collar should end at the "collar end" markings on pattern. Sew a seam.
7. Fold SLEEVES where indicated, with right sides touching (Figure A). Sew seam from bottom of SLEEVE to armpit and then to the bottom of the coat. Clip curves, particularly around the armpit. Repeat on other side.
8. Fold over remaining open edges. Top stitch from bottom of coat up the front opening, along the underside of the collar, down the other side of front opening, and then meet stitching on bottom of coat.
9. Take crocheted cotton thread or braided sewing thread and insert end into one of the dots indicated on the FRONT pattern piece. Repeat with other end of thread into other dot on pattern. Tie a double knot on the inside of the coat, leaving the loop a little loose to accommodate the belt.
10. Fold BELT in half and press with iron. Fold each of those halves inward and press (Figure C). Take pointed edges and fold inward. Press with iron. Top stitch around border of belt.
11. Apply desired buttons, rivets, or iron-on metal appliqué to front of coat. If desired, add to sleeves. Add buckle to belt.

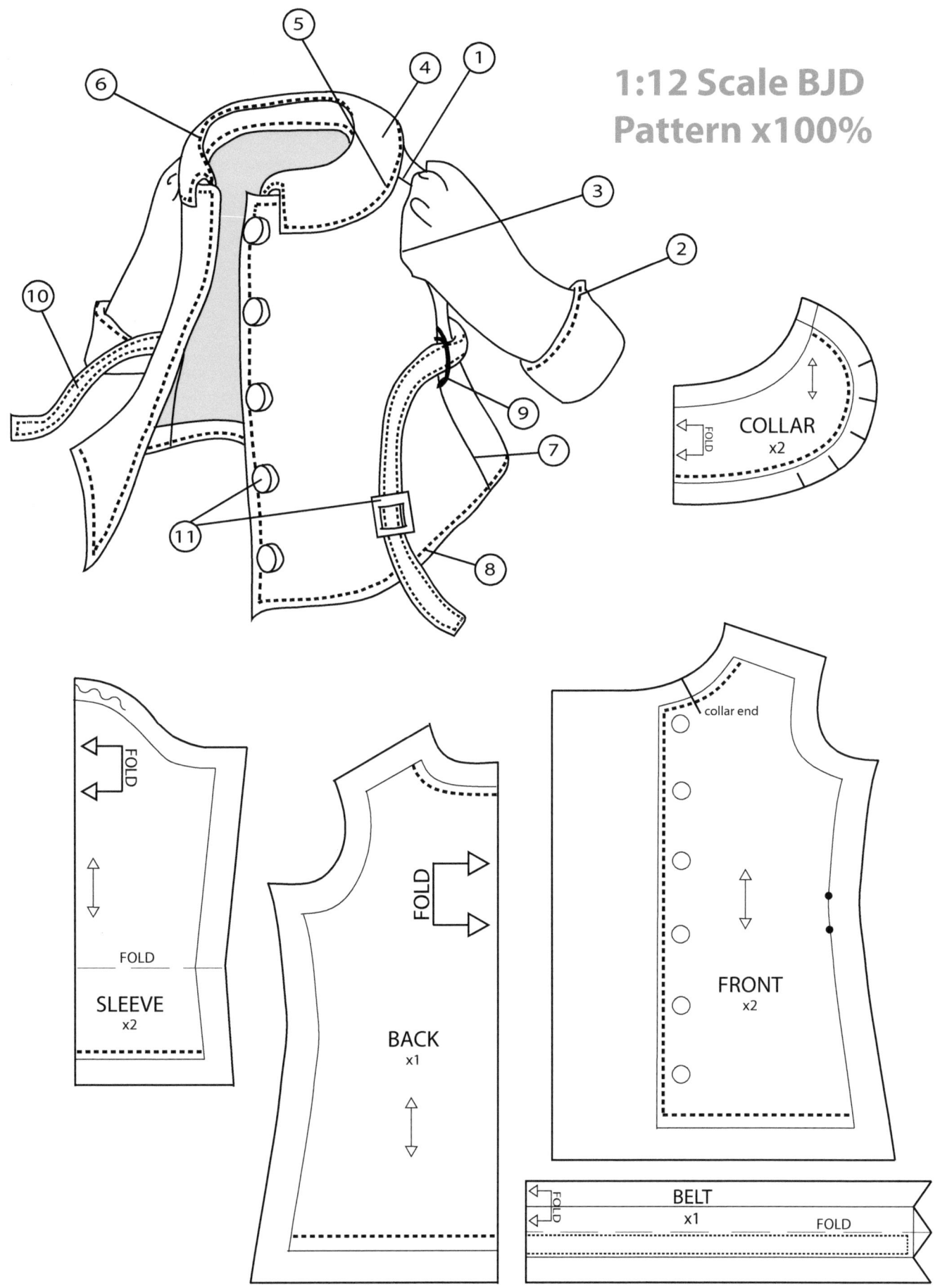

momoko Pattern x100%

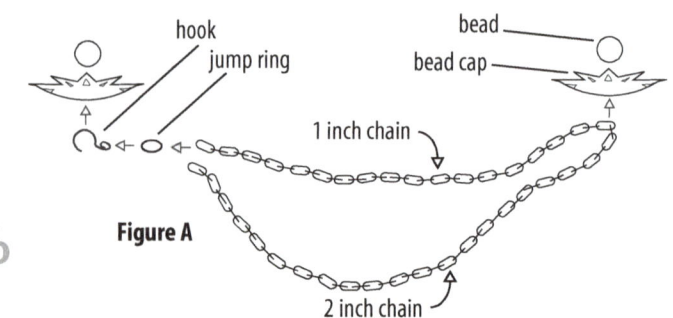

Figure A

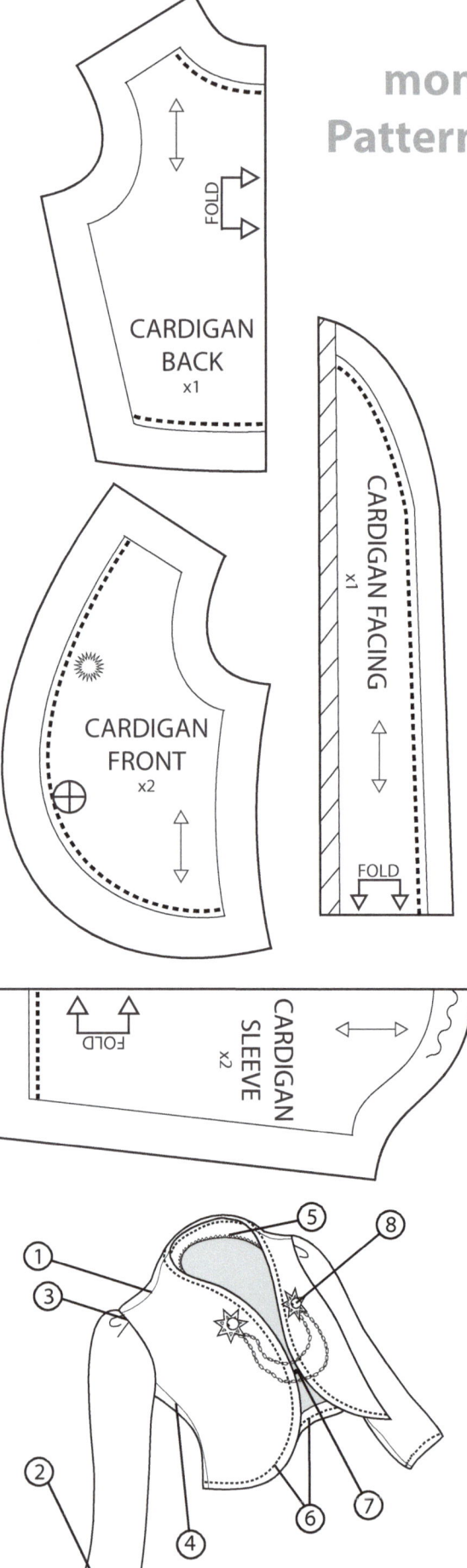

Cardigan:

Photos on pages 14-15.

Pattern Pieces:
CARDIGAN FRONT x2, CARDIGAN BACK x1, CARDIGAN SLEEVE x2, and CARDIGAN FACING x1.

Supplies:
Sewing pattern basics (See pages 42-43)
Needle and thread
Hook-and-eye closure
Measuring tape
Bead caps
Beads
Jewelry hook
Jewelry jump ring
Chain
Crimp pliers with cutter

Steps:
Before following the steps outlined in the diagram, cut enough of each pattern piece for this cardigan. A thin fabric is recommended for the facing.

1. Sew shoulder seams of CARDIGAN FRONT pieces to CARDIGAN BACK with the right sides together. Press seams open.
2. Fold bottom side of the CARDIGAN SLEEVE over and top stitch. Repeat for other CARDIGAN SLEEVE.
3. Make small gather in area indicated on CARDIGAN SLEEVE. Ease upper CARDIGAN SLEEVE into each armhole using sewing pins or basting stitch. Make sure right sides are together. Sew seam and repeat for other CARDIGAN SLEEVE.
4. Sew seam from bottom of CARDIGAN SLEEVE to armpit and then to the bottom of the garment. Clip curves, particularly at armpit area. Repeat on other side.
5. Sew a zigzag stitch along indicated area of CARDIGAN FACING. Trim excess fabric for a clean edge.
6. With right sides together, sew a seam of CARDIGAN FACING to CARDIGAN FRONT pieces and neck of CARDIGAN BACK. Facing piece will reach all of edge except bottom of CARDIGAN BACK piece. Fold inside out and top stitch around entire edging, including bottom of CARDIGAN BACK.
7. Hand sew hook-and-eye closure on the inside of the cardigan where indicated on the pattern. To make stitching not visible on the outside, sew closure to facing, not outside of jacket.
8. With 3 inches of chain, measure out 1 inch in the chain and sew that link onto cardigan with bead cap and bead (Figure A). Combine open chain links together with jewelry hook on a jump ring. Sew remaining bead cap and bead onto other side of cardigan.

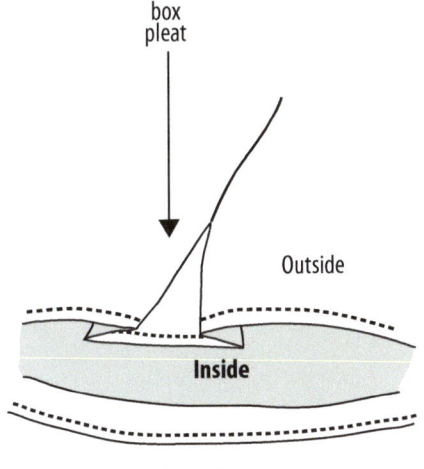

Figure B

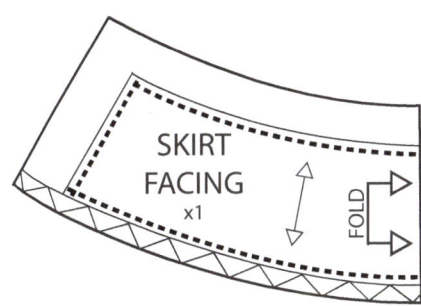

momoko Pattern x100%

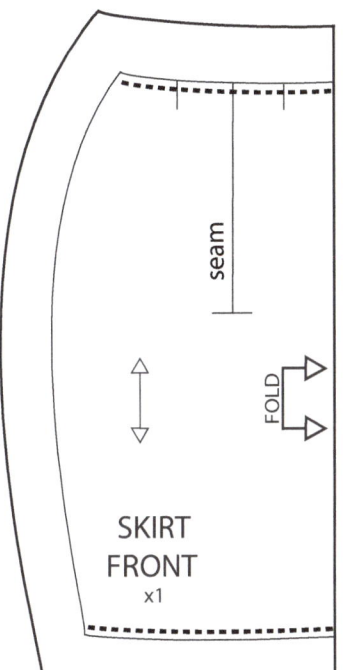
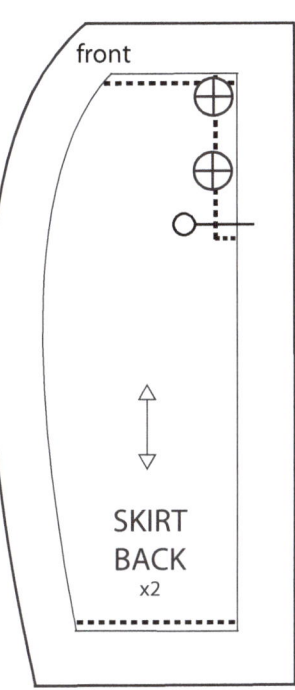

Skirt:

Photos on pages 14-15.

Pattern Pieces:
SKIRT FRONT x1, SKIRT BACK x2, and SKIRT FACING x1

Supplies:
Sewing pattern basics (See pages 42-43)
Needle and thread
Bead-and-loop closure

Steps:
Before following the steps outlined in the diagram, cut enough of each pattern piece for this skirt. A thin fabric is recommended for the facing.

1. Sew seam down SKIRT FRONT piece and SKIRT BACK piece marked "front" with right sides together. Repeat with other SKIRT BACK piece to other side of SKIRT FRONT. Press seams open.
2. Fold bottom side of skirt over and top stitch.
3. Fold skirt in half vertically and sew a seam where indicated on the SKIRT FRONT piece. Press open to make a box pleat on inside of skirt (Figure B).
4. Sew a zigzag stitch along indicated area of SKIRT FACING. Trim excess fabric for a clean edge.
5. With right sides together, sew seam of top of garment to top of SKIRT FACING. Turn inside out and top stitch skirt and facing.
6. With right sides together, sew seam from bottom of skirt to ○—— point on pattern. Turn inside out. See pages 45-47 for a bead-and-loop *Closures* guide.

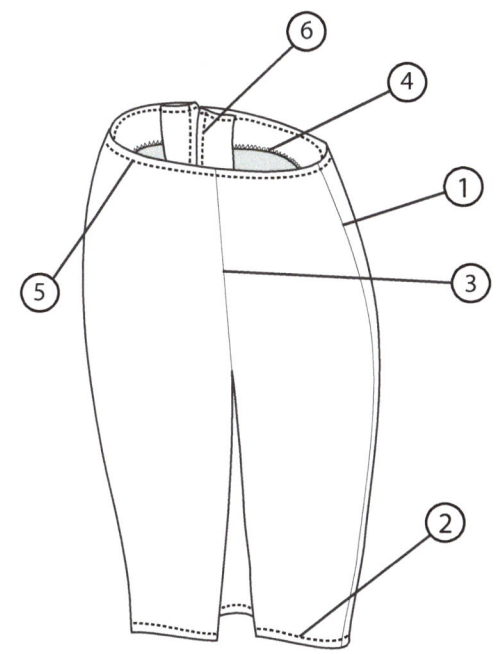

65

momoko

momoko Pattern x100%

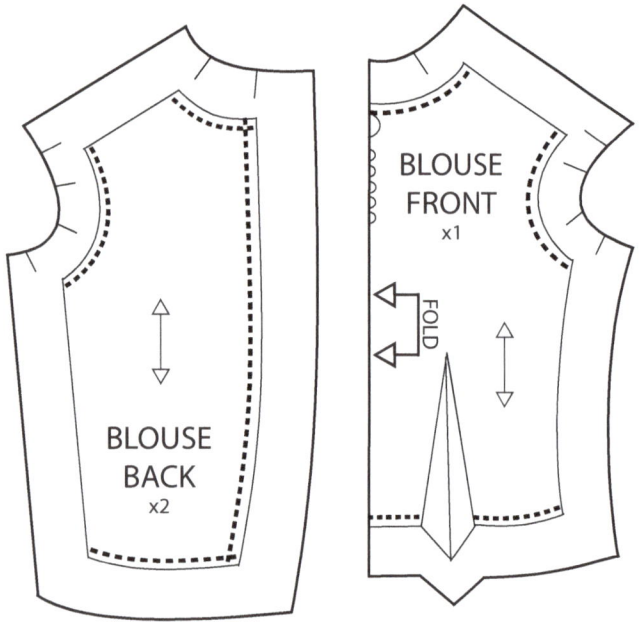

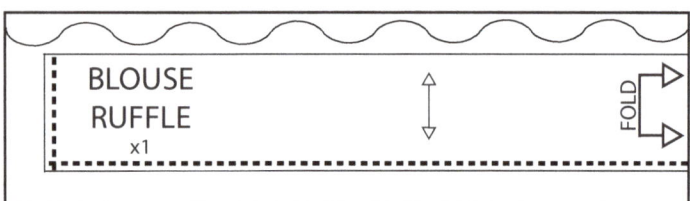

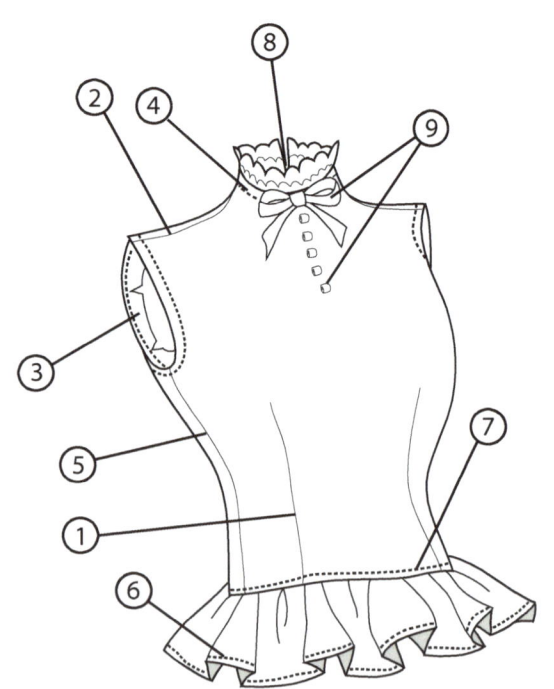

Blouse:

Photos on pages 14-15.

Pattern Pieces:
BLOUSE FRONT x1, BLOUSE BACK x2, and BLOUSE RUFFLE x1

Supplies:
Sewing pattern basics (See pages 42-43)
Needle and thread
Seed beads
Ribbon (3 mm or less)
Lace trim
Hook-and-loop closure tape

Steps:
Before following the steps outlined in the diagram, cut enough of each pattern piece for this blouse.

1. Make darts on either side of BLOUSE FRONT piece by folding right side together and sewing along outer seams of dart. Repeat on other side of BLOUSE FRONT piece. Press darts down towards center.
2. Sew shoulder seams of BLOUSE FRONT piece to BLOUSE BACK pieces with the right sides together. Press seams open.
3. After clipping pattern where indicated, fold over armholes using pins or a basting stitch. Top stitch.
4. Cut enough lace for the entire length of the neck opening at its seam. Clip pattern in neck opening where indicated. Using either a basting stitch or pins, fold over neck opening and attach lace to backside of neck opening. Top stitch with one or two rows of stitches.
5. With right sides together, sew seam of BLOUSE BACK and BLOUSE FRONT pieces from armhole to bottom of garment. Repeat on other side.
6. Fold over bottom of BLOUSE RUFFLE and top stitch.
7. On the BLOUSE RUFFLE, gather where indicated until gather is the length of the bottom of the blouse. With right sides together, pin gathered fabric every 1/2 inch to 1 inch to the blouse. Sew seam. Fold seam of ruffle and blouse pieces up and top stitch along the blouse garment.
8. Fold over open edge of back pieces and sew hook-and-loop closure tape onto entire length of back of garment. See pages 45-47 for a hook-and-loop tape *Closures* guide.
9. Make a bow with 3 mm (or less) ribbon. Hand sew onto garment along with 5 seed beads.

1:4 Scale Ball-Jointed Dolls

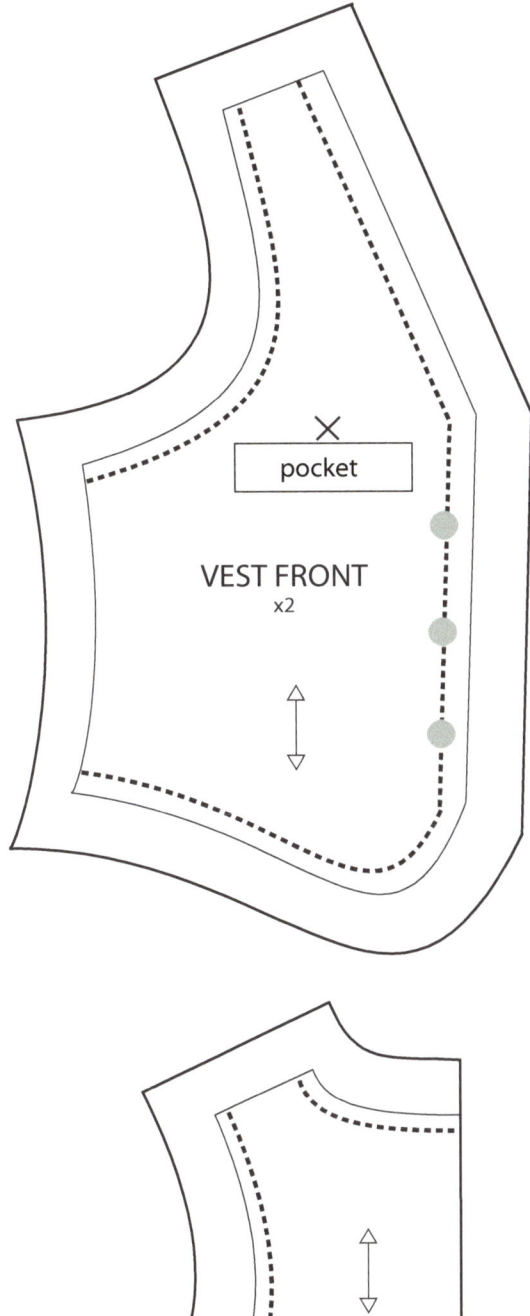

Vest:

Photos on pages 20 and 22-23.

Pattern Pieces:
VEST FRONT x2, VEST BACK x1, and VEST POCKET x1

Supplies:
Sewing pattern basics (See pages 42-43)
Needle and thread
Chain (about 2 inches long)
Buttons, rivets, or iron-on metal applique
Fabric flower or embroidered flower applique

Steps:
Before following the steps outlined in the diagram, cut enough of each pattern piece for this vest.

1. Sew shoulder seams of VEST FRONT pieces to VEST BACK with the right sides together. Press seams open.
2. Fold arm opening over and hold in place with pins or a basting stitch. Top stitch. Repeat for other arm opening.
3. With right sides together, sew seam of sides of VEST FRONT pieces to VEST BACK. Turn inside out.
4. Fold over remaining raw edges and hold in place with pins or a basting stitch. Top stitch from bottom of VEST BACK piece, around to the front of vest, up to the neck opening, back down the other VEST FRONT piece, and then back to the VEST BACK bottom.
5. Fold over top of VEST POCKET and top stitch. Fold over sides and bottom of VEST POCKET and place in indicated area on right VEST FRONT piece. Top stitch over sides and bottom of pocket to hold in place on vest.
6. Place desired buttons, rivets, or iron-on metal applique where indicated on right-sided VEST FRONT piece.
7. Using a needle and thread, sew ends of chain to vest at area marked "X" on pattern. Over the ends of chain, stitch fabric flower or embroidered flower applique onto vest.

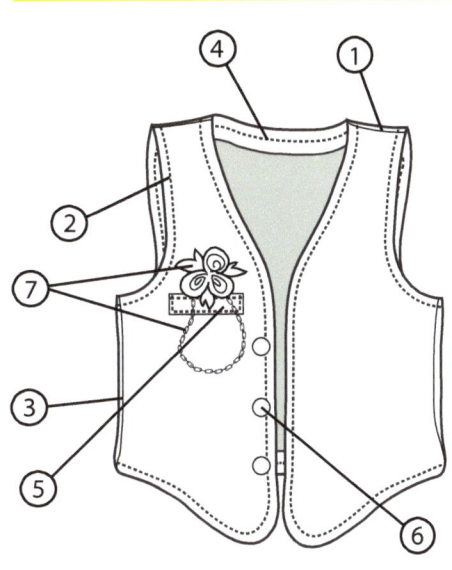

1:4 Scale BJD Pattern x100%

1:4 Scale Ball-Jointed Dolls

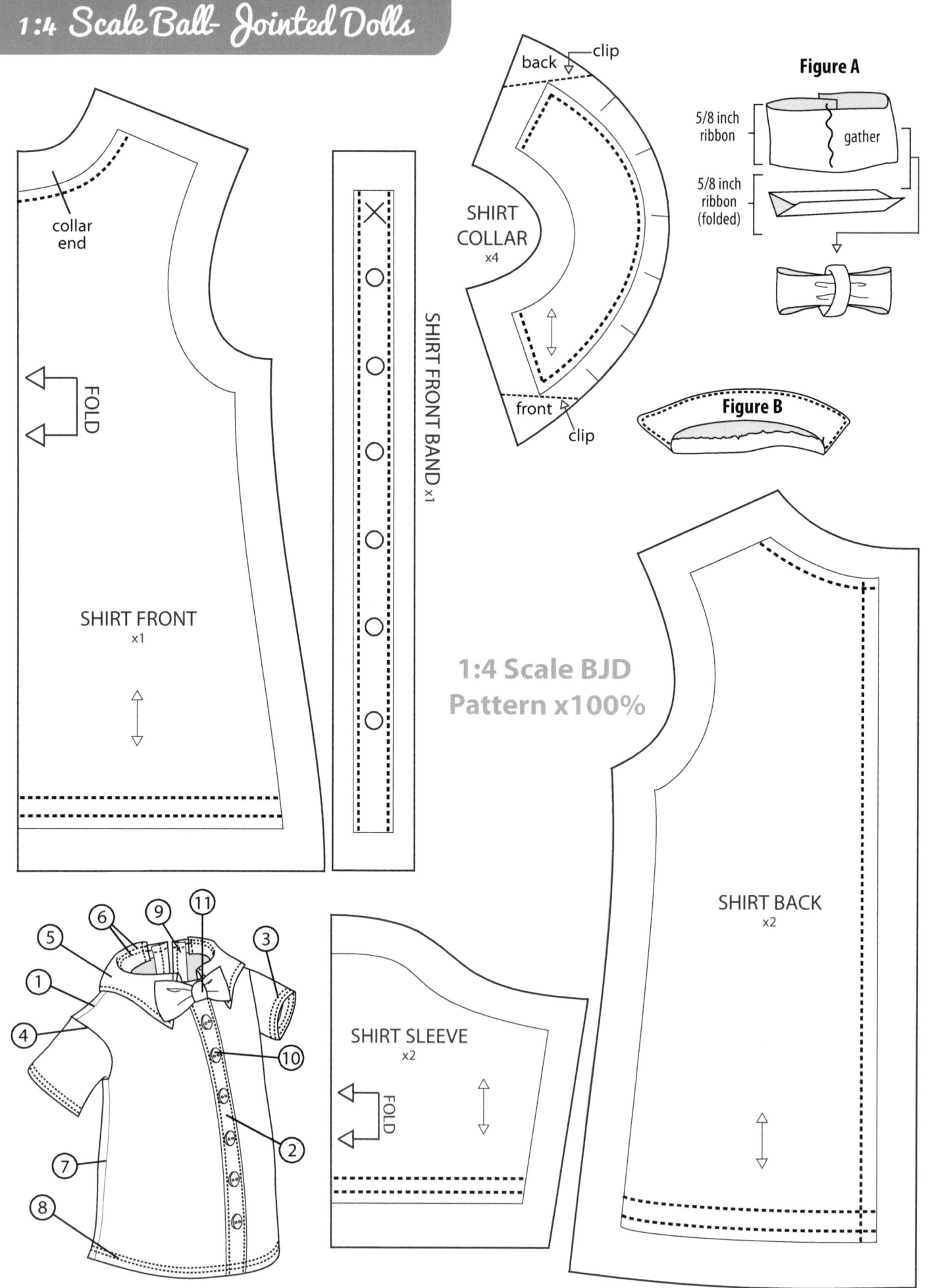

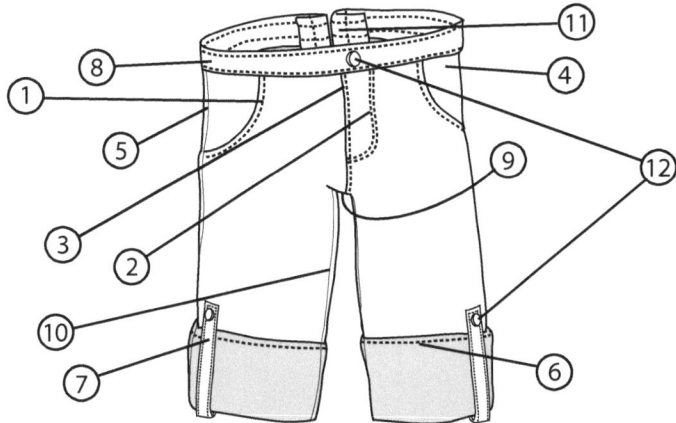

1:4 Scale Ball-Jointed Dolls

Shirt:

Photos on pages 20 and 22-23.

Pattern Pieces:
SHIRT FRONT x1, SHIRT BACK x2, SHIRT SLEEVE x2, SHIRT COLLAR x4, and SHIRT FRONT BAND x1

Supplies:
Sewing pattern basics (See pages 42-43)
Buttons
Ribbon (5/8 inch)
Hook-and-loop closure tape

Steps:
Before following the steps outlined in the diagram, cut enough of each pattern piece for this shirt.

1. Sew shoulder seams of SHIRT FRONT to SHIRT BACK pieces with the right sides together. Press seams open.
2. Fold long edges back on SHIRT FRONT BAND piece and press. Place vertically in middle of SHIRT FRONT piece and top stitch around border of SHIRT FRONT BAND.
3. Fold bottom side of each SHIRT SLEEVE over and top stitch with two rows of stitches.
4. Ease upper SHIRT SLEEVE into each armhole using sewing pins or basting stitch. Make sure right sides are together. Sew seam and repeat for other SHIRT SLEEVE.
5. With right sides together, sew seam down back side, outer curve, and front side of SHIRT COLLAR. Make sure to leave open area to turn inside out. Clip curves as pictured on collar pattern. Also, clip corners of seams to make corners of collar look clean and less bulky. Turn inside out. If possible, turn open end of SHIRT COLLAR inside and press (Figure B). This will leave a clean edge in the shirt, although is optional. Top stitch seam of SHIRT COLLAR.
6. With the underside of the SHIRT COLLAR facing the right side of the SHIRT BACK and SHIRT FRONT pieces, ease the pieces using pins or basting stitch. The collar should end at the "collar end" markings on pattern. Sew a seam. Fold collar and neck opening down and top stitch over these on the shirt neck opening. This will help hold the collar down.
7. With right sides together, sew seam from bottom of SHIRT SLEEVE to armpit and then to the bottom of the garment. Clip curves, especially under armpit. Repeat on other side.
8. Fold over bottom of shirt and top stitch two rows of stitches.
9. Fold over open edge of back pieces and sew hook-and-loop closure into back of garment. See pages 45-47 for a helpful hook-and-loop *Closures* guide.
10. Hand sew buttons where indicated on pattern.
11. Cut approximately 3 inches of 5/8 inch wide ribbon. Fold raw edges back and have them overlap about 1/4 inch. Make a gather in the middle of the ribbon (Figure A). Cut approximately 1-1/4 inches of same 5/8 inch wide ribbon. Fold long finished edges in and wrap ribbon around middle of gathered area on first ribbon. Hand sew back to hold bow together and then sew onto shirt.

Pants:

Photos on pages 20 and 22-23.

Pattern Pieces:
PANTS FRONT x2, PANTS BACK x2, PANTS BELT x1, PANTS POCKET x2, and PANTS STRAP x2 (pattern on page 70)

Supplies:
Sewing pattern basics (See pages 42-43)
Needle and thread
Buttons or iron-on metal applique
Bead-and-loop closure

Steps:
Before following the steps outlined in the diagram, cut enough of each pattern piece for these pants. Pants are meant for a doll with waist circumference of approximately 7-1/2 to 8 inches. This pattern works best with a fabric backside that is pleasing to the eye, since the backside of the fabric will be folded over and seen on the bottom of the pants.

1. Fold over pockets on PANTS FRONT pieces using pins of a basting stitch. Clip curves to make folding easier. Top stitch.
2. On left PANTS FRONT piece, top stitch two rows of stitches indicated on pattern as "decorative stitch."
3. With right sides together, sew seam of rise in PANTS FRONT pieces. Press open. Top stitch over left PANTS FRONT piece.
4. Sew a zigzag stitch along indicated area of PANTS POCKET. Trim excess fabric for a clean edge. Place pocket on inside of pants pocket opening with curved part of PANTS POCKET piece being covered by the PANTS FRONT piece. PANTS POCKET right side should be facing the backside of the PANTS FRONT piece. Pin or use a stitch to keep each pocket in place.
5. With right sides together, sew seam of long length of corresponding PANTS FRONT and PANTS BACK pieces. Make sure PANTS POCKET piece is attached when sewing seam. Repeat with other side. Press seams open.
6. Fold bottom of pants over, exposing the back side. Fold over one more time at indicated area on pattern. The back side of the fabric should be facing the front side of the pants. Top stitch along top of folded area.
7. Fold long edges of PANTS STRAP pieces back and press. Top stitch along both edges of PANTS STRAP pieces. Fold in half and place on pants where indicated with an "X." Hand stitch through both ends of strap and pants to hold into place.
8. With right sides together, sew seam of top of pants to PANTS BELT. Fold BELT over seam and top stitch around front side of belt.
9. With right sides together, sew seam of rise in PANTS BACK pieces to ——O point on pattern. Press seams open.
10. With right sides together, sew seam from bottom of one pant leg, up to the rise, and down to the other pant leg. Turn inside out.
11. See pages 45-47 for a bead-and-loop *Closures* guide.
12. Add buttons or rivets to areas indicated on PANTS BELT and PANTS STRAP pieces.

1:4 Scale Ball-Jointed Dolls

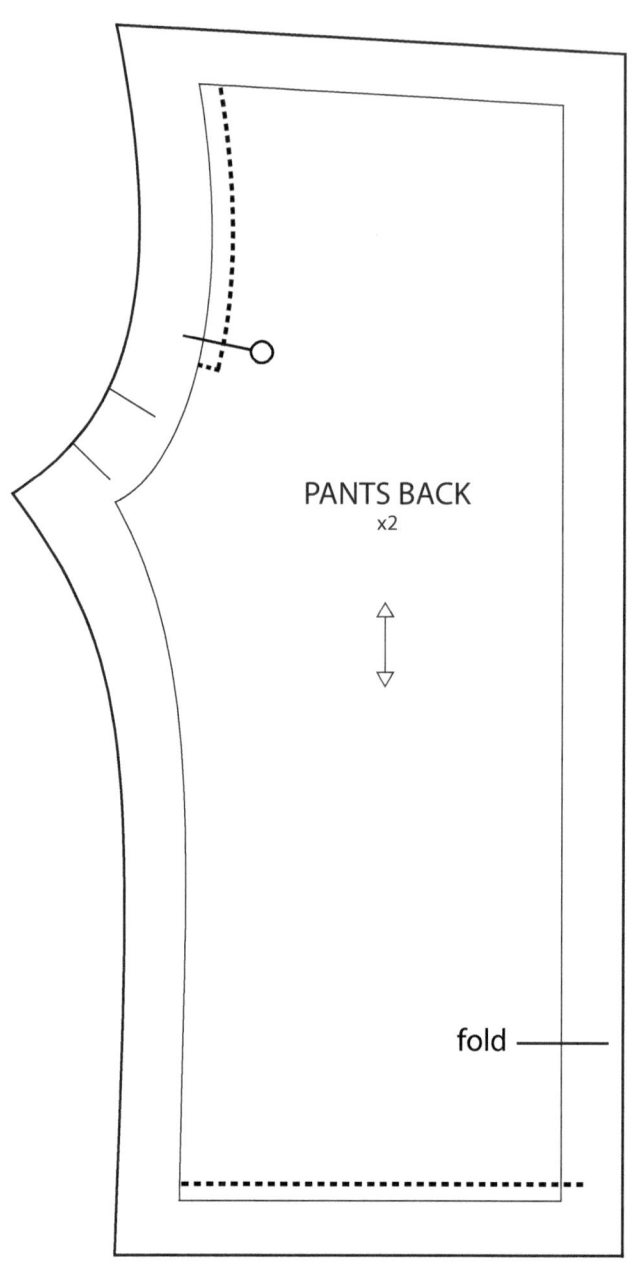

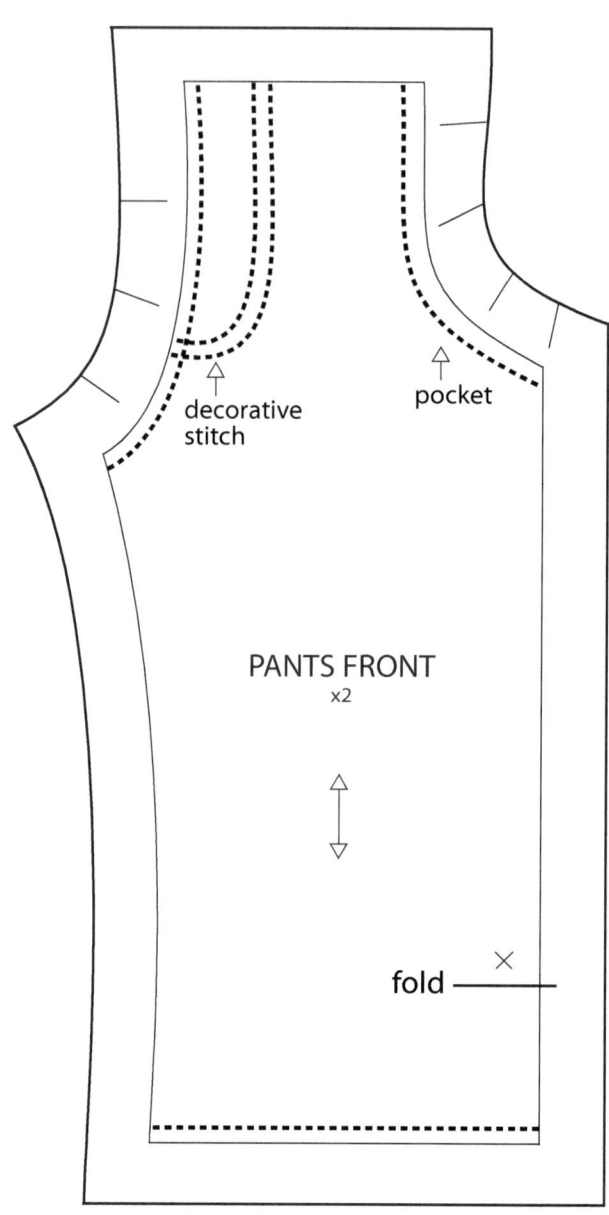

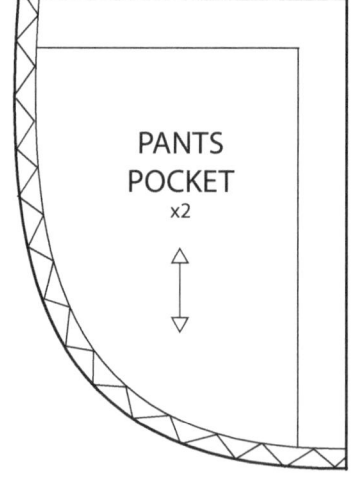

1:4 Scale BJD Pattern x100%

1:4 Scale Ball-Jointed Dolls

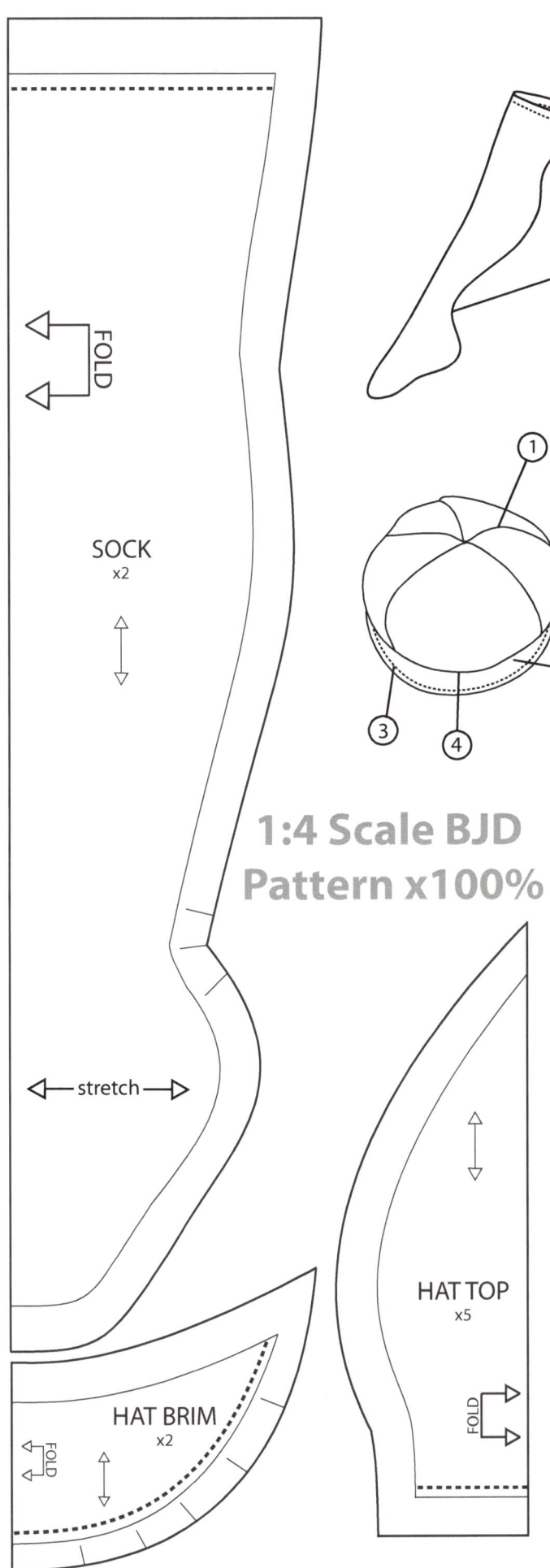

1:4 Scale BJD Pattern x100%

Socks:

Photos on pages 20 and 22-23.

Pattern Pieces:
SOCK x2

Supplies:
Sewing pattern basics (See pages 42-43)

Steps:
Before following the steps outlined in the diagram, cut enough of each pattern piece for these socks. Knit/stretchable fabric is recommended for this pattern.

1. Fold top side of the SOCK over and top stitch. Repeat for other SOCK piece.
2. With right sides together sew seam from top of SOCK, down to the heel and through to the fold in the SOCK. Clip curves where indicated on pattern. Turn inside out and repeat for other SOCK piece.

Hat:

Photos on pages 20 and 22-23.

Pattern Pieces:
HAT TOP x5 and HAT BRIM x2

Supplies:
Sewing pattern basics (See pages 42-43)

Steps:
Before following the steps outlined in the diagram, cut enough of each pattern piece for this hat. If a different fabric is desired for underside of hat brim, substitute one piece of HAT BRIM in desired fabric.

1. With right sides together, sew a seam of long side of HAT TOP pieces. Repeat with all pieces until they are joined together.
2. With right sides together, sew seam of outer rim of both HAT BRIM pieces. Clip curves, turn inside out, and press.
3. Top stitch along seam edge of brim.
4. With right sides together, pin brim to opening of HAT TOP pieces. The middle of the brim should be in the middle of one of the HAT TOP pieces. Sew a seam over the hat brim.
5. Fold over remaining raw edges as well as seam of brim and HAT TOP pieces. Top stitch over entire opening of hat.

Misaki & Poppy Parker

Misaki/Poppy Parker Pattern x100%

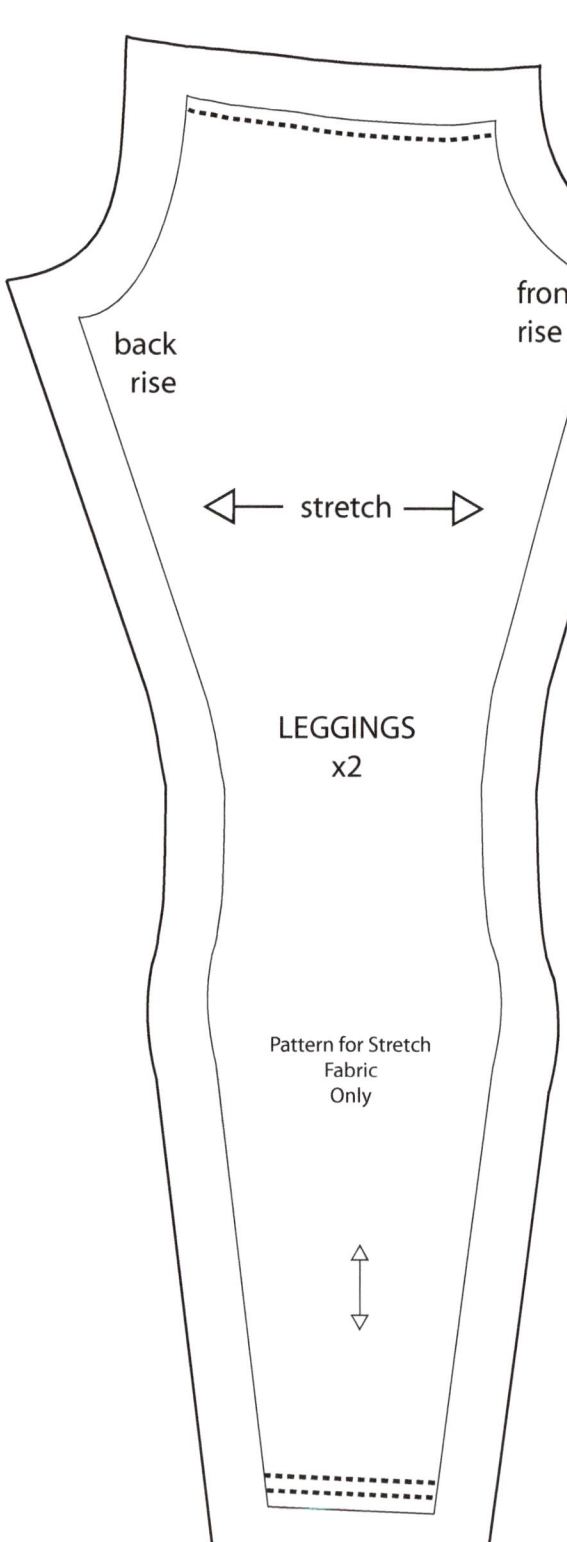

Leggings:

Photo on page 2 and 25.

Pattern Pieces:
LEGGINGS x2

Supplies:
Sewing pattern basics (See pages 42-43)

Steps:
Before following the steps outlined in the diagram, cut enough of each pattern piece for these leggings. The pattern is specifically meant for knit/stretch fabric.

1. With right sides together of both LEGGINGS pieces, sew seam of front rise. If fabric is iron-friendly, press seams open.
2. Fold top of leggings over and top stitch.
3. Fold the bottom side of each pant leg over and top stitch with two rows of stitches.
4. With right sides together of both LEGGINGS pieces, sew seam of back rise.
5. With right sides together, sew seam from bottom of one pant leg up to the rise and then down the other pant leg. Turn inside out.

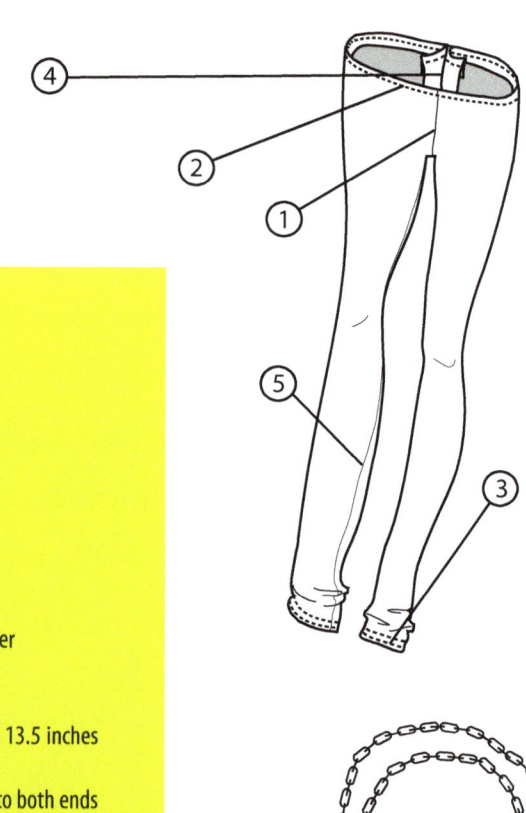

Waist Chain:

Photo on page 2.

Supplies:
Chain
Jump rings
Charms
Measuring tape
Crimp pliers with cutter

Steps:
1. Cut approximately 13.5 inches of chain.
2. Attach jump rings to both ends of chain. Do not close.
3. Attach charm to both ends of chain in the jump ring. Close jump rings. Wrap around waist of doll and tie a loose knot in the chain.

Misaki & Poppy Parker

Off-Shoulder Top:

Photo on page 2 and 25.

Pattern Pieces:
FRONT x1, BACK x2, and SLEEVE x2

Supplies:
Sewing pattern basics (See pages 42-43)
Bead-and-loop closure (optional, see below)

Steps:
Before following the steps outlined in the diagram, cut enough of each pattern piece for this pattern. The pattern will not require snaps in the back if using a knit/stretchable fabric like jersey.

1. Fold bottom side of each SLEEVE over and top stitch with two rows of stitches.
2. Sew seam of front side of SLEEVE and arm opening of FRONT together with right sides together. Repeat with other SLEEVE on other arm opening of FRONT. Press seams open.
3. Sew seam of back side of SLEEVE and arm opening of BACK together with right sides together. Repeat with other SLEEVE and BACK pieces. Press seams open.
4. Fold the top opening of garment over and top stitch with two rows of stitches.
5. With right sides together, sew seam from bottom of one armhole opening up to the armpit then down to join the FRONT and BACK pieces. Clip curves, particularly around armpit area. Repeat with other side. Turn sleeves inside out.
6. Fold the bottom of garment over and top stitch with two rows of stitches.
7. If using stretchable fabric, with right sides together, sew seam along entire back side of garment and turn inside out. If using less stretchable fabric, with right sides together, sew seam from bottom of garment to —O point on pattern. Turn inside out. See pages 45-47 for a bead-and-loop *Closures* guide.

Misaki/Poppy Parker Pattern x100%

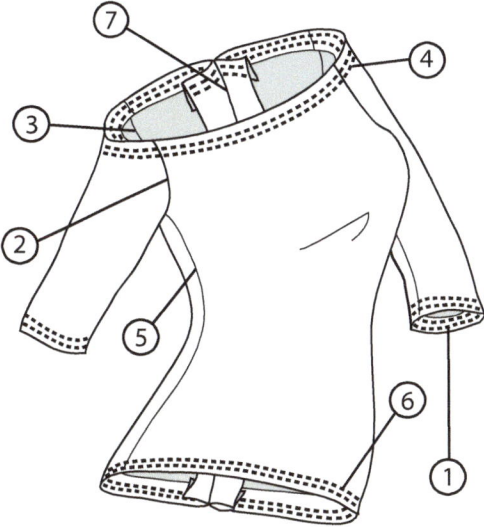

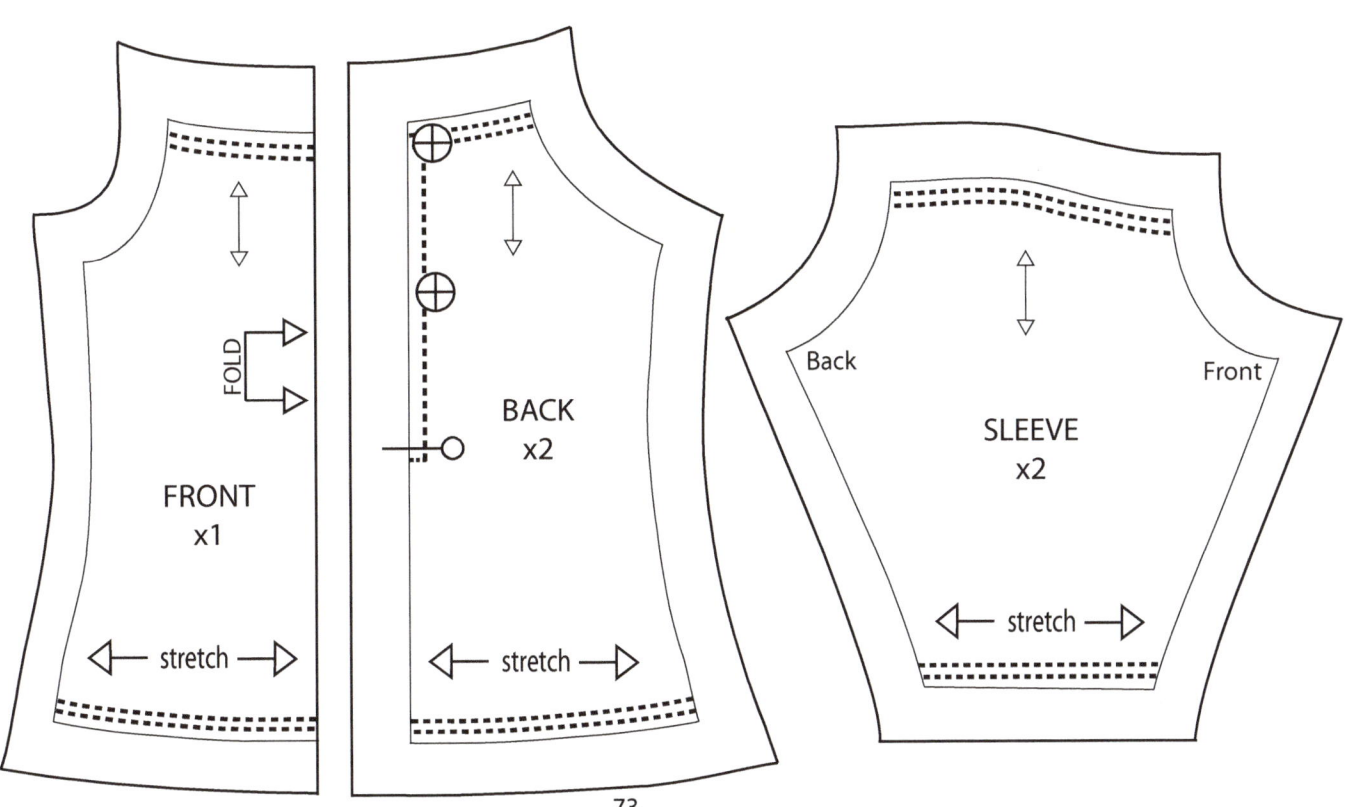

1:4 Scale Ball-Jointed Dolls

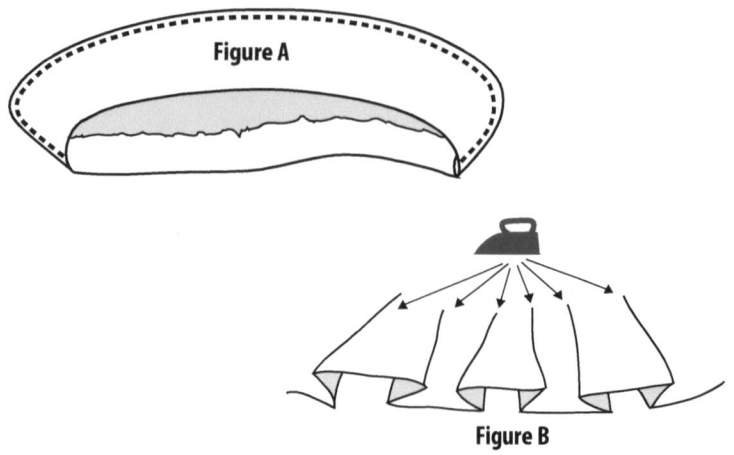

Figure A

Figure B

Dress:

Photos on page 4 and cover.

Pattern Pieces:
FRONT x1, BACK x2, SLEEVE x2, SKIRT x1, and COLLAR x4 (pattern on pages 76-77)

Supplies:
Sewing pattern basics (See pages 42-43)
Needle and thread
Lace trim
Ribbon (3 mm and 3/8 inch)
Beads or buttons
Hook-and-loop closure tape

Steps:
Before following the steps outlined in the diagram, cut enough of each pattern piece for this dress.

1. Cut enough lace for the length of the bottom of the SLEEVE pattern. Fold bottom side of the SLEEVE over and top stitch with lace pinned to the back of the fabric. Lace should be held in place with the top stitch. Repeat for other cut SLEEVE pattern.
2. Sew shoulder seams of FRONT to BACK with the right sides together. Press seams open.
3. Ease upper SLEEVE into armhole using sewing pins or basting stitch. Make sure right sides are together. Sew seam and repeat for other SLEEVE.
4. With right sides together, sew seam from outer curve to other outer curve of COLLAR. Make sure to leave open area to turn inside out. Clip curves as pictured on collar pattern. Turn inside out. Press with iron.
5. If possible, turn open end of COLLAR inside and press (Figure A). This will leave a clean edge in the garment, although is optional. Top stitch seam of COLLAR.
6. With the underside of the COLLAR facing the right side (not back side of fabric) of the BACK and FRONT pieces, ease the pieces using pins or basting stitch to sew a seam. Turn seams down onto FRONT and BACK pieces. Top stitch along underside of collar.
7. Sew seam from bottom of SLEEVE to armpit and then to the bottom of the garment. Clip curves, particularly around armpit. Repeat on other side.
8. Fold bottom side of SKIRT over and top stitch.
9. Fold skirt over at markings indicated on SKIRT pattern. Press with iron to make box pleats (Figure B).
10. With right sides together, pin top of SKIRT to bottom of FRONT and BACK garment. Sew seam. Fold seam of SKIRT up and top stitch along the FRONT and BACK garment.
11. Cut enough 3/8 inch wide ribbon for length of garment. Top stitch ribbon onto garment.
12. With right sides together, sew seam from bottom of back of SKIRT up to ⊶ point on the BACK pattern. Turn inside out. See pages 45-47 for a hook-and-loop tape *Closures* guide.
13. Hand sew ribbon made into a bow in between collar pieces. Hand sew beads/buttons just below the bow.

1:4 Scale Ball-Jointed Dolls

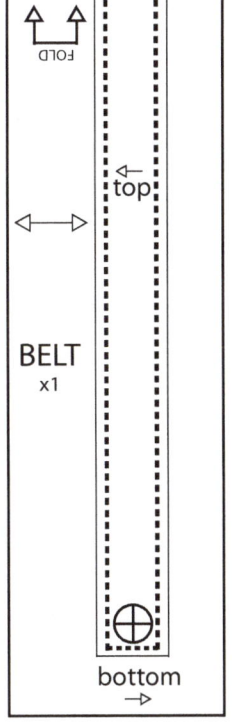

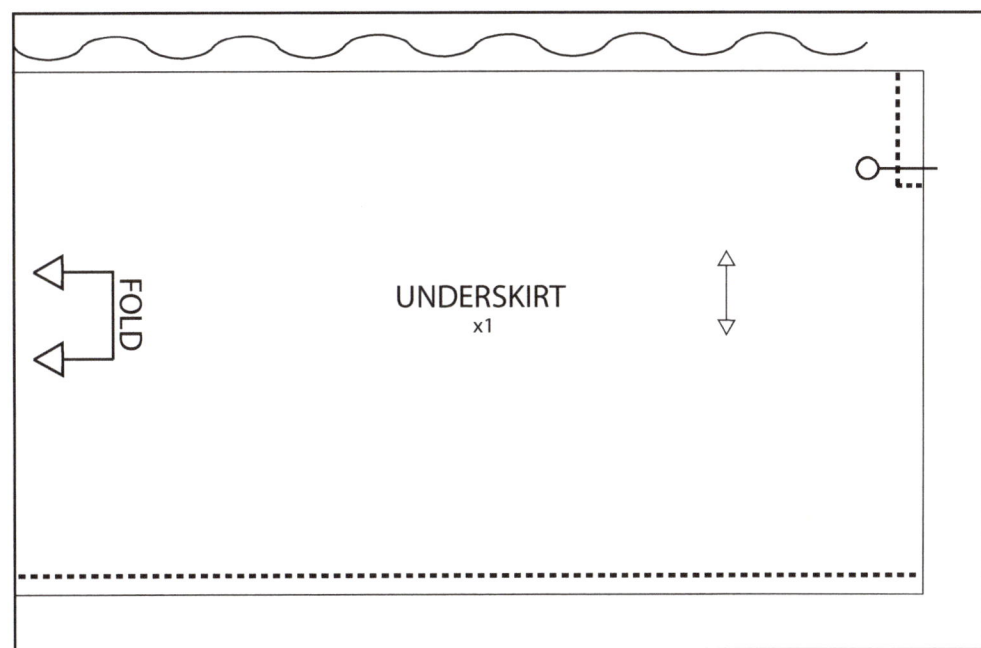

1:4 Scale BJD Pattern x100%

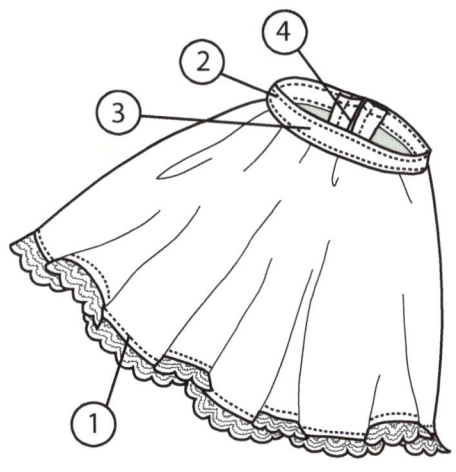

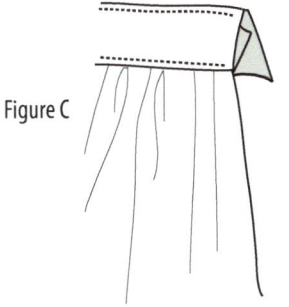

Figure C

Underskirt:

Photos on page 4 and cover.

Pattern Pieces:
UNDERSKIRT x1 and BELT x1

Supplies:
Sewing pattern basics (See pages 42-43)
Needle and thread
Lace trim
Bead-and-loop closure

Steps:
Before following the steps outlined in the diagram, cut enough of each pattern piece for this underskirt. Skirt is meant for a doll with waist circumference of approximately 7-1/2 inches. Add or subtract appropriate amount to BELT pattern, if necessary.

1. Cut enough lace for the length of the long side of the UNDERSKIRT pattern. Fold bottom side of UNDERSKIRT over and top stitch with lace pinned to the back of the fabric. Lace should be held in place with the top stitch.
2. On the UNDERSKIRT, gather where indicated until gather is the length of the BELT. With right sides together, pin gathered fabric every 1/2 inch to inch to the BELT. Sew seam.
3. Fold BELT over seam and top stitch top and bottom of belt (Figure C).
4. With right sides together, sew seam from bottom of back of UNDERSKIRT up to ◯──── point on pattern. Turn inside out. See pages 45-47 for a loop-and-bead *Closures* guide.

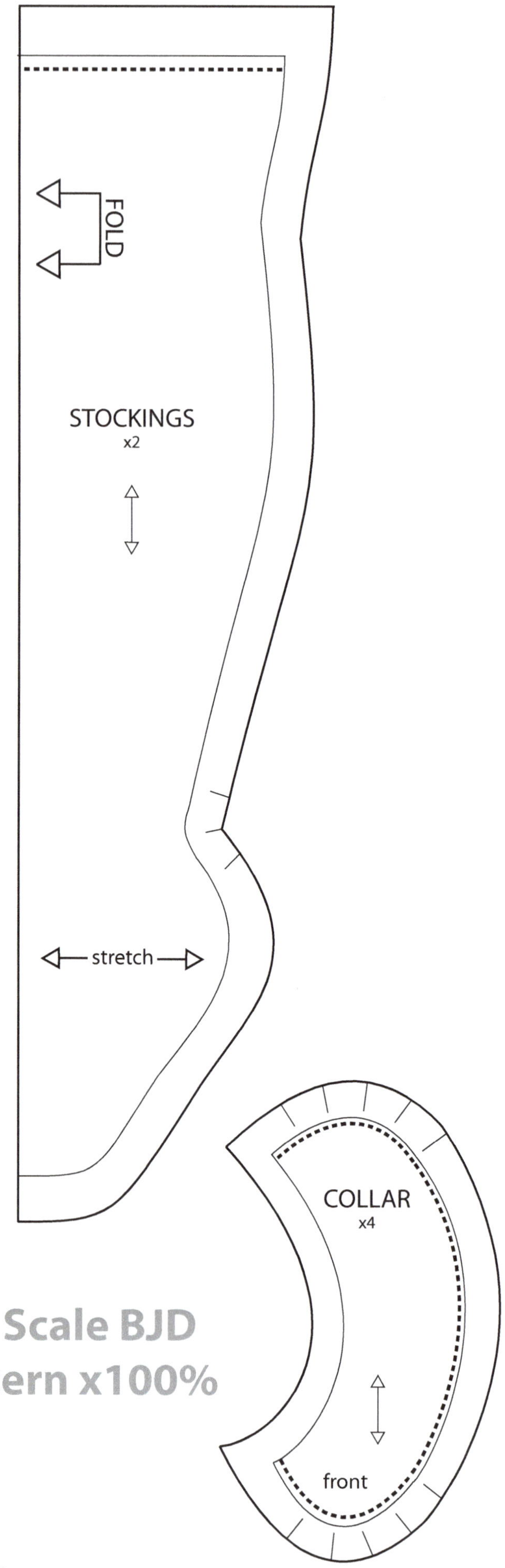

1:4 Scale Ball-Jointed Dolls

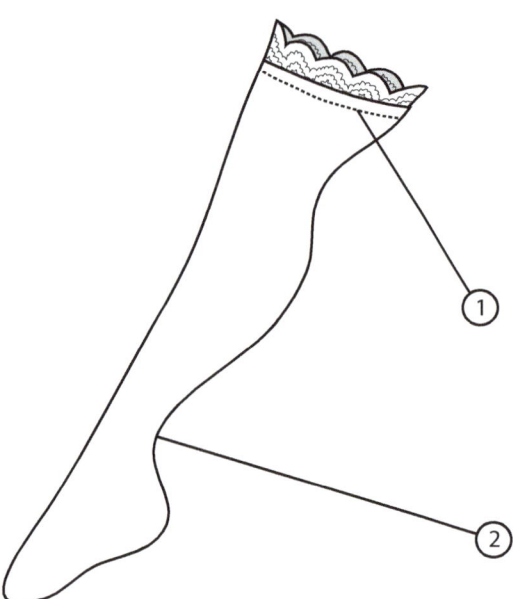

Stockings:

Photos on page 4 and cover.

Pattern Pieces:
STOCKINGS x2

Supplies:
Sewing pattern basics (See pages 26-27)
Lace

Steps:
Before following the steps outlined in the diagram, cut enough of each pattern piece for these stockings.

1. Cut enough lace for the length of the top of the STOCKINGS pattern. Fold top side of the STOCKINGS over and top stitch with lace pinned to the back of the fabric. Lace should be held in place with the top stitch. Repeat for other cut STOCKINGS pattern.
2. With right sides together sew seam from top of STOCKINGS through the lace, down to the calf and through to the fold in the foot. Clip curves where indicated on pattern. Turn inside out and repeat for other cut STOCKINGS pattern.

STOCKINGS x2 — FOLD — stretch

COLLAR x4 — front

1:4 Scale BJD Pattern x100%

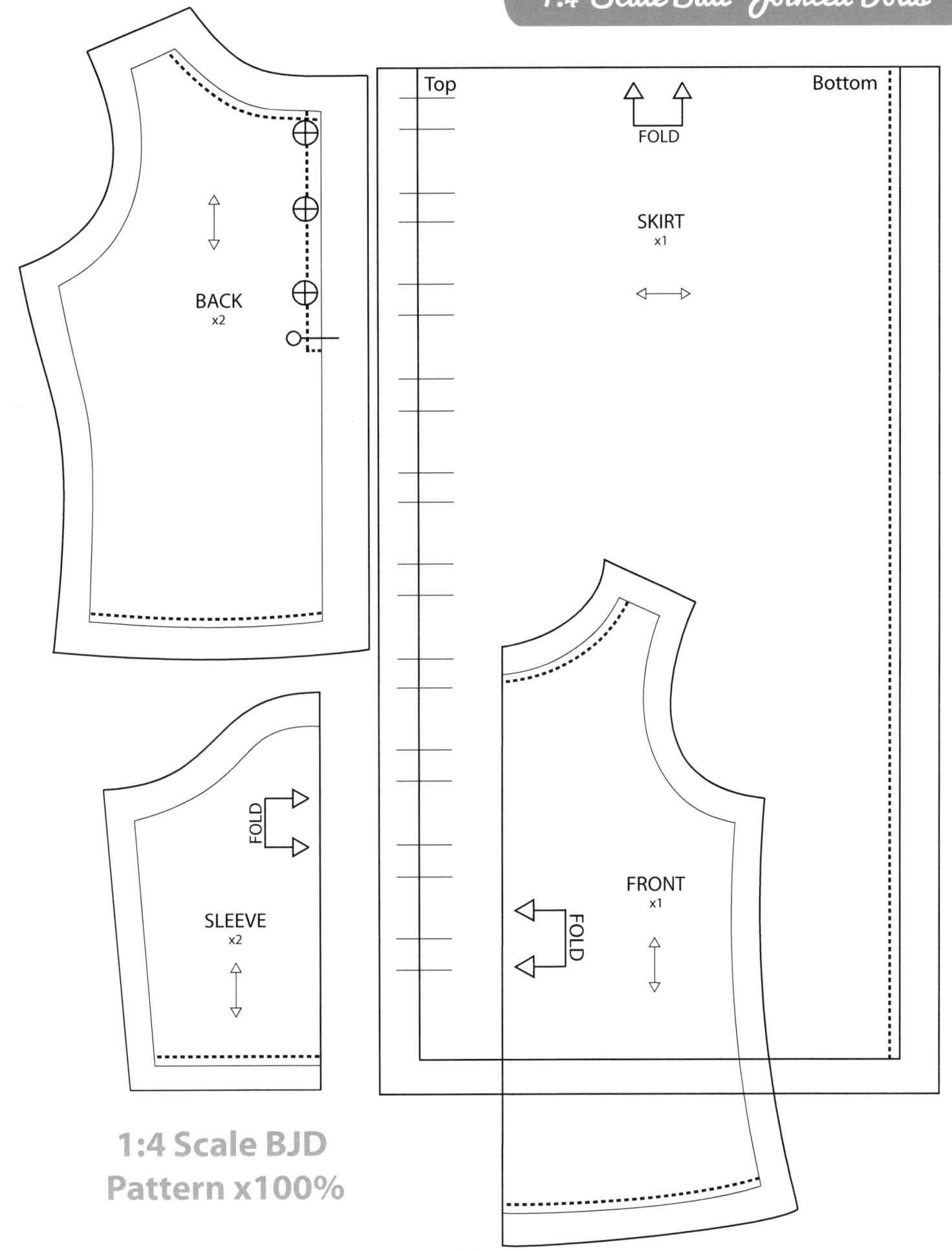

momoko

momoko Pattern x100%

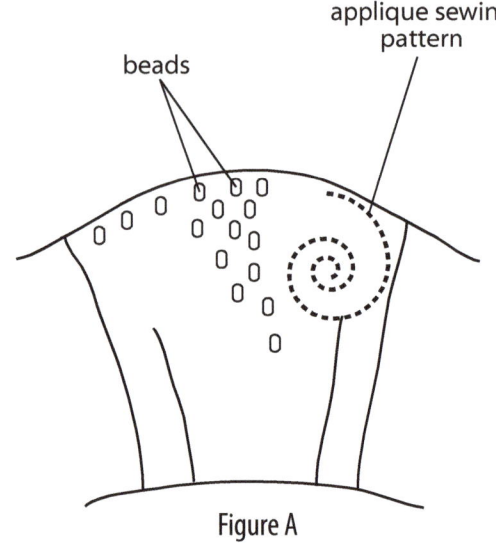

Figure A

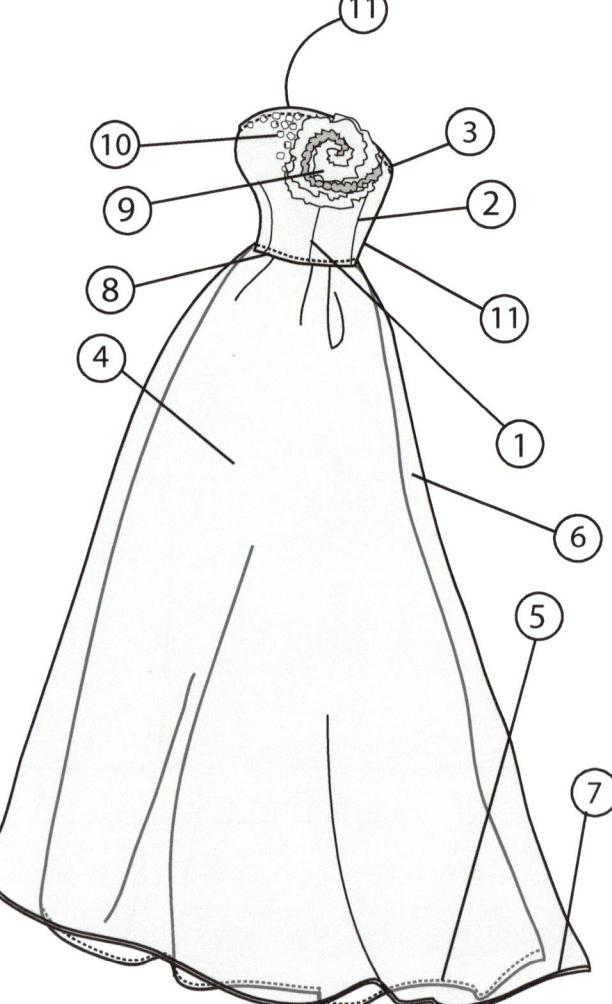

Dress:

Photo on page 3.

Pattern Pieces:

TOP FRONT x1 for underlining and tulle, TOP BACK x2 for underlining and tulle, SKIRT FRONT x1 for underlining and tulle, SKIRT BACK x2 for underlining and tulle, and TULLE FLOWER x1

Supplies:

Sewing pattern basics (See pages 42-43)
Needle and thread
Bead-and-loop closures
Measuring tape
Seed beads
Ribbon (3 mm)

Steps:

Before following the steps outlined in the diagram, cut enough of each pattern piece for this dress. Tulle is used as the outside layer of the entire dress as well as for the flower applique. Pattern is meant for multiple layers of fabric and may be slightly too large if very thin single layers of fabric are used.

1. With tulle on front side of underlining fabric, make darts on either side of TOP FRONT piece by folding right side together and sewing along outer seams of dart. Repeat on other side of TOP FRONT piece. Press darts down center.
2. With tulle on front side of underlining fabric, sew seam of TOP BACK to TOP FRONT with right sides together. Repeat with other TOP BACK piece. Press seams.
3. Fold top of garment over and top stitch.
4. Using underlining fabric only, sew seam of SKIRT FRONT piece to a SKIRT BACK piece with right sides together. Repeat with other SKIRT BACK piece to other side of SKIRT FRONT piece. Press seams.
5. Fold over bottom of skirt pieces and top stitch where indicated on pattern.
6. Using tulle fabric only, sew seam of SKIRT FRONT piece to a SKIRT BACK piece with right sides together. Repeat with other SKIRT BACK piece to other side of SKIRT FRONT piece. Trim excess or uneven seams to give a very clean minimal edge since it will be seen through the fabric.
7. Sew a zigzag stitch along bottom of tulle skirt pieces. Trim excess tulle for a clean edge.
8. With tulle on front side of underlining fabric, gather top of skirt until it is the length of the bottom of the corset. With right sides together, pin every 1/2 inch and sew seam over skirt and corset pieces. Fold seam of skirt and corset pieces up and top stitch along the corset garment.
9. Make a gather stitch through the entire length of the TULLE FLOWER piece. Gather should measure approximately 4 inches. Repeat gathering with 8 inches of 3mm ribbon. Ribbon gather should measure approximately 2-3/4 inches in length. Hand sew tulle and ribbon gathers in a spiral pattern onto dress (Figure A).
10. Hand sew seed beads on front side of dress (Figure A).
11. With right sides together, sew seam from bottom of back of skirt up to ⟶O point on pattern. Turn inside out. See pages 45-47 for a bead-and-loop *Closures* guide.

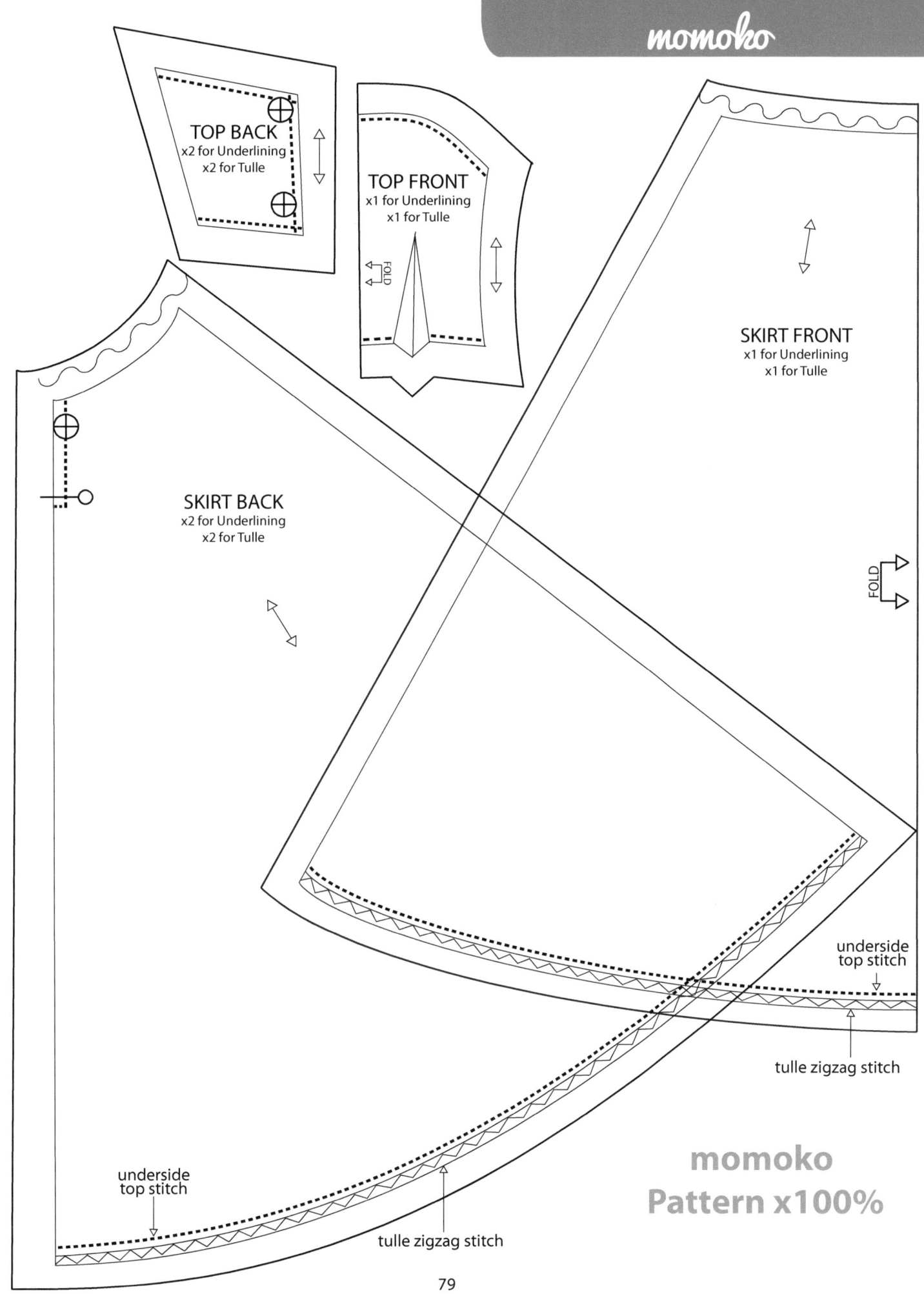

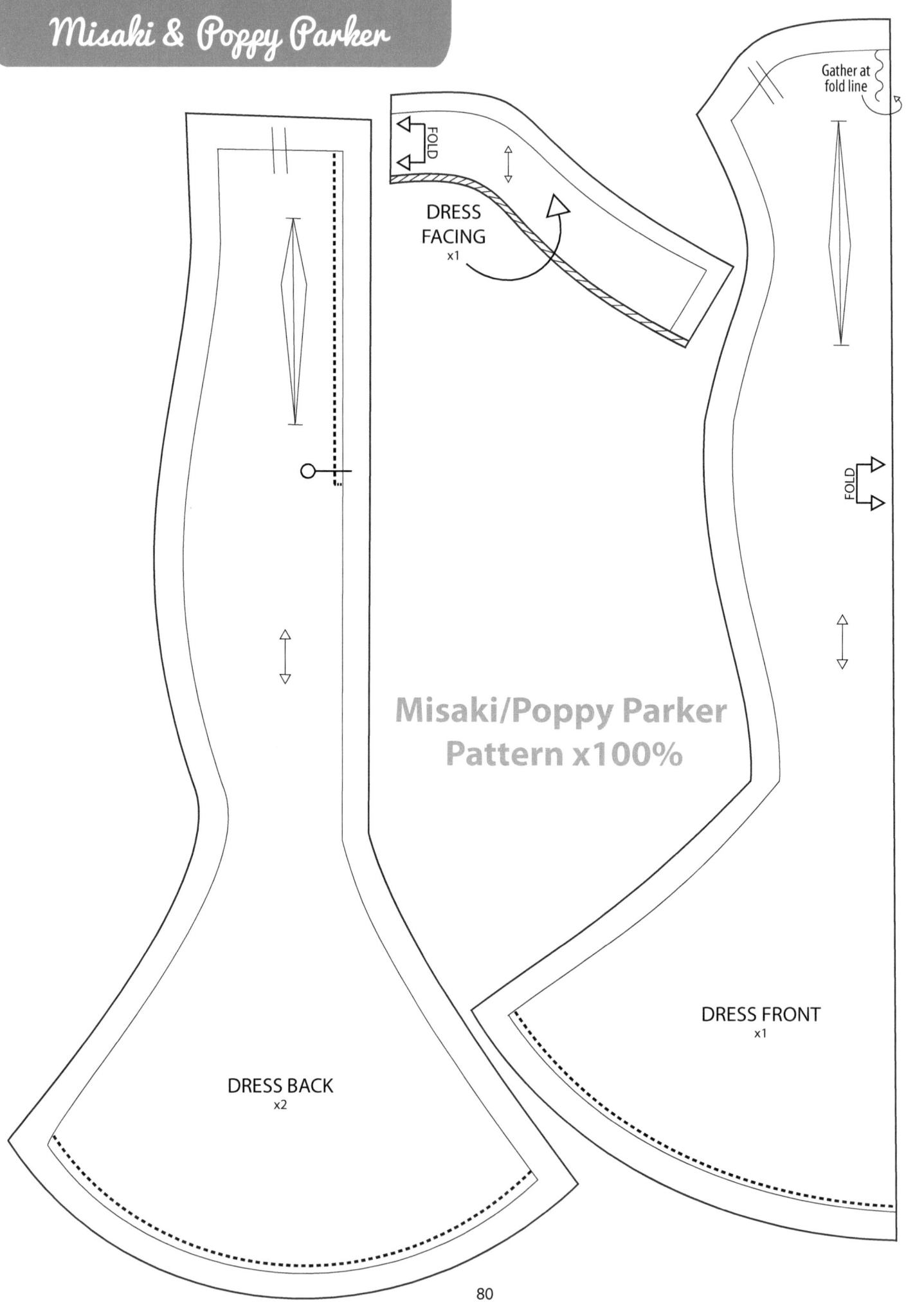

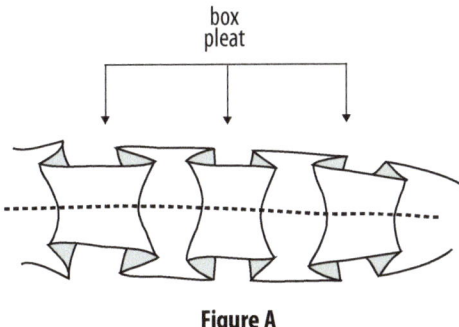

Figure A

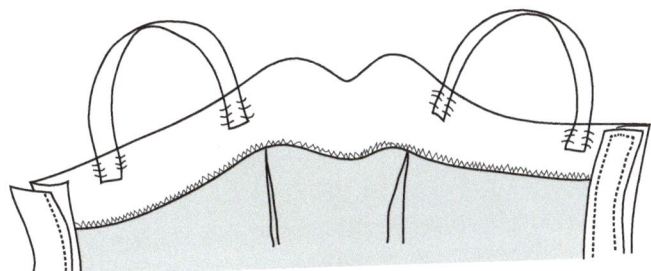

Misaki & Poppy Parker

Figure B

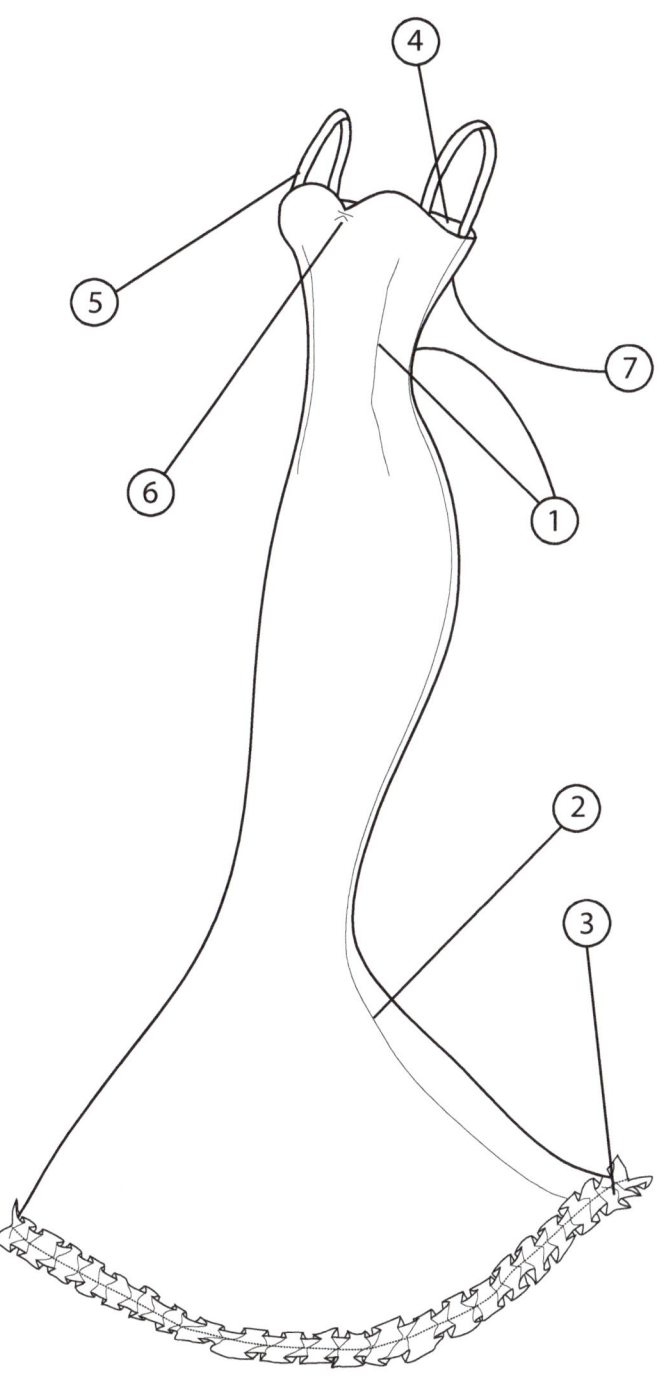

Dress:

Photos on pages 16-17.

Pattern Pieces:
DRESS FRONT x1, DRESS BACK x2, and DRESS FACING x1

Supplies:
Sewing pattern basics (See pages 42-43)
Needle and thread
Hook-and-loop closure tape
Ribbon (5/8 inch and 3 mm)
Measuring tape

Steps:
Before following the steps outlined in the diagram, cut enough of each pattern piece for this dress. A thin fabric is best for the facing.

1. Make darts on either side of DRESS FRONT piece by folding right side together and sewing along outer seams of dart. Repeat on other side of DRESS FRONT piece. Press darts down center. Repeat with darts on DRESS BACK pieces.
2. With right sides together, sew seam of DRESS FRONT to a DRESS BACK piece. Repeat with other DRESS BACK piece to other side of DRESS FRONT. Press seams.
3. Fold over bottom side of dress and top stitch. Using approximately 36 inches of 5/8 inch ribbon, ruffle ribbon by making box pleats along hem (Figure A). Hold pleats in place with pins or a basting stitch. Top stitch over center of box pleats.
4. Sew a zigzag stitch along indicated area of DRESS FACING. Trim excess fabric for a clean edge. With right sides together, sew a seam of top of DRESS FACING to top of DRESS FRONT and DRESS BACK pieces. Fold inside out and press.
5. Cut two pieces of 3 mm ribbon about 3 inches long. Make straps for dress with ribbon by hand-stitching the ribbon onto the facing of the dress. It is recommended to check the strap length on a doll before sewing straps onto garment. Use Figure B as a guide for stitching straps to facing.
6. With a needle and thread, hand sew a gather on the front of the dress for a sweetheart bustline.
7. With right sides together, sew seam from bottom of back of dress up to o— point on pattern. Turn inside out. See pages 45-47 for a hook-and-loop tape *Closures* guide.

1:12 Scale Ball-Jointed Dolls

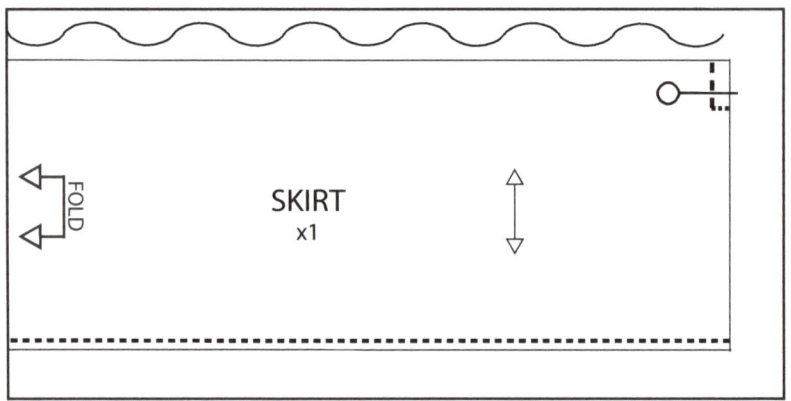

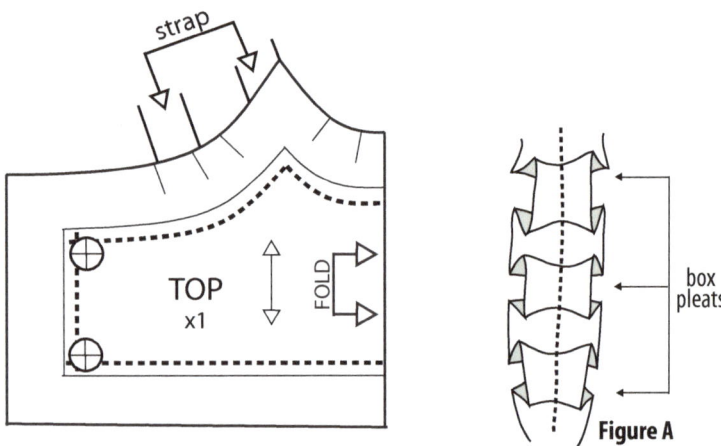

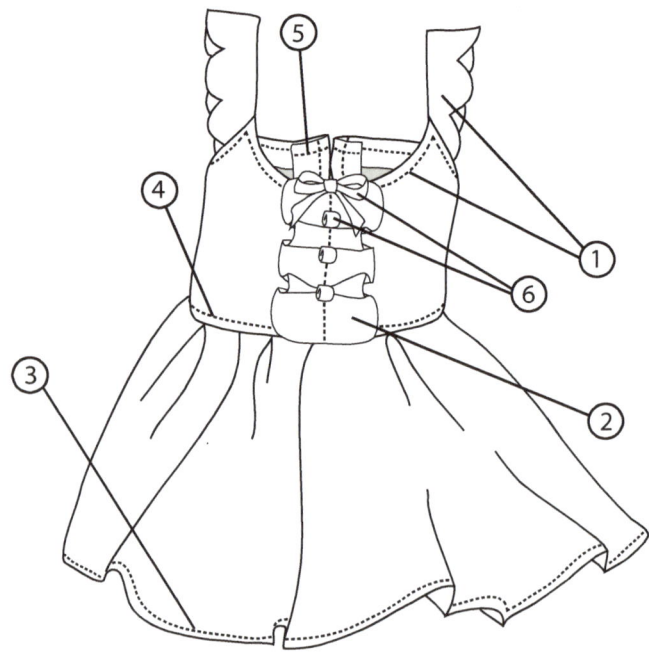

1:12 Scale BJD Pattern x100%

Dress:

Photos on pages 12-13.

Pattern Pieces:
TOP x1 and SKIRT x1

Supplies:
Sewing pattern basics (See pages 42-43)
Measuring tape
Bead-and-loop closure
Lace trim
Seed beads
Ribbon (3 mm or smaller)

Steps:
Before following the steps outlined in the diagram, cut enough of each pattern piece for this dress.

1. Fold over upper side of TOP and pin. Cut two pieces of approximately 2-1/4 inches lace trim for straps. Pin strap pieces in place as indicated on pattern. Double check length of straps for doll. Top stitch over TOP and lace trim straps.
2. Cut approximately 2 inches of lace trim and make a ruffle over the middle to the TOP piece using pinned box pleats (Figure A). Top stitch directly down middle of ruffle.
3. Fold over bottom of SKIRT and top stitch.
4. Gather top of SKIRT until it is the length of the bottom of the TOP piece. With right sides together, pin in place about once every 1/2 inch. Sew a seam. Fold SKIRT and TOP pieces up and top stitch over TOP piece.
5. With right sides together, sew seam from bottom of dress to ⊙—— point on pattern. Turn inside out. See pages 45-47 for a bead-and-loop *Closures* guide.
6. Hand sew seed beads and ribbon where indicated.

Socks:

Photo on page 13.

Pattern Pieces:
SOCK x2

Supplies:
Sewing pattern basics (See pages 42-43)

Steps:
Before following the steps outlined in the diagram, cut enough of each pattern piece for these socks. Knit/stretchable fabric is recommended for this pattern.

1. Fold top side of the SOCK over and top stitch. Repeat for other SOCK piece.
2. With right sides together sew seam from top of SOCK, down to the heel and through to the fold in the SOCK. Clip curves where indicated on pattern. Turn inside out and repeat for other SOCK piece.

1:12 Scale Ball-Jointed Dolls

1:12 Scale BJD Pattern x100%

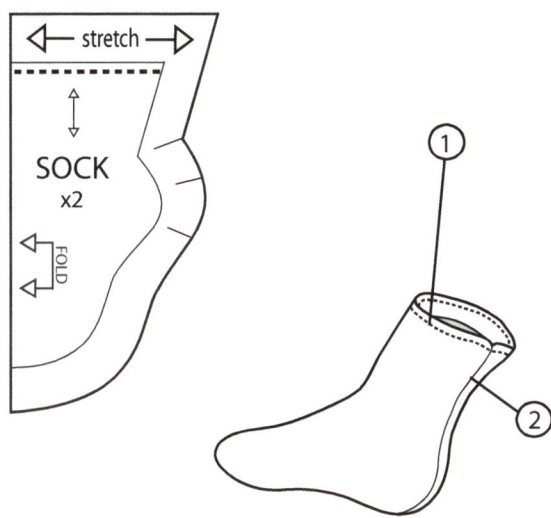

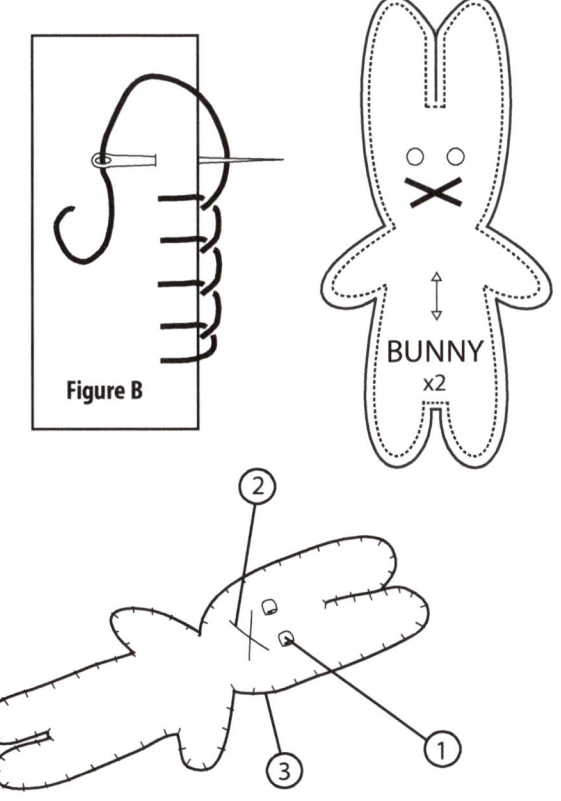

Figure B

Stuffed Bunny:

Photo on page 12.

Pattern Pieces:
BUNNY x2

Supplies:
Sewing pattern basics (See pages 42-43)
Needle and embroidery thread
Seed beads

Steps:
Before following the steps outlined in the diagram, cut enough of each pattern piece for this stuffed bunny. Felt is recommended. Leftover felt scraps from cutting out pattern are used as stuffing. A sewing machine is not required.

1. On one BUNNY piece, hand sew both seed beads, where indicated. These will be the eyes of the stuffed bunny.
2. On the same BUNNY piece, hand sew an "X" shape as shown.
3. Take leftover scrap felt and lightly stuff in between BUNNY pieces. Using embroidery thread, do a basic blanket stitch all the way around the stuffed bunny (Figure B).

1:4 Scale Ball-Jointed Dolls

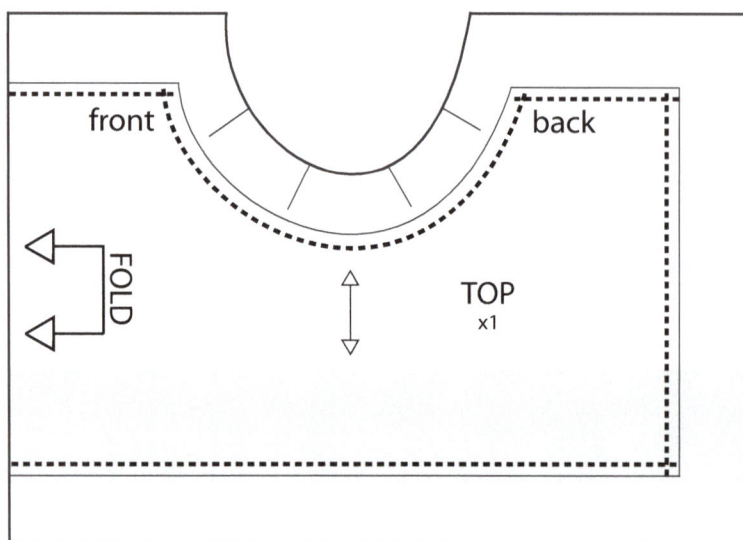

1:4 Scale BJD Pattern x100%

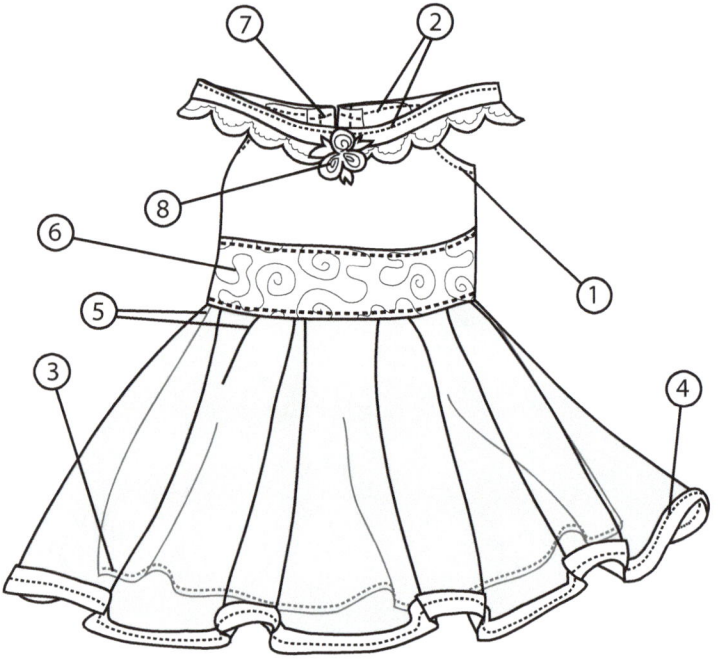

Figure A

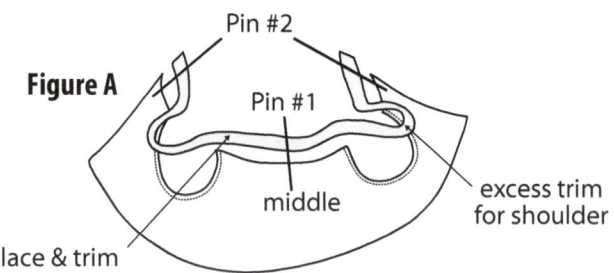

Dress:

Photos on pages 20-22.

Pattern Pieces:
TOP x1, SKIRT x1, TULLE SKIRT x1, and ARMHOLE FACING x2

Supplies:
Sewing pattern basics (See pages 42-43)
Needle and thread
Embroidered trim
Double fold bias tape (1/4 inch)
Lace trim with ribbon
Flower applique
Hook-and-loop closure tape

Steps:
Before following the steps outlined in the diagram, cut enough of each pattern piece for this dress. Tulle fabric is recommended for the TULLE SKIRT piece. Note: Parts of this pattern require a little more than 1 yard of fabric.

1. Sew a zigzag stitch along indicated area of ARMHOLE FACING. Trim excess fabric for a clean edge. With right sides together, sew seam of ARMHOLE FACING to the armhole of the TOP piece. Make sure "front" and "back" parts of each pattern piece correspond. Clip curved edges. Turn inside out and top stitch TOP and ARMHOLE FACING. Repeat for other side.

2. Measure out enough lace trim for off-shoulder dress straps. Be sure to test length on doll. The pattern in this book on a Peak's Woods Fairy of Bugs body measured approximately 9.5 inches. Measure out same amount of ribbon to go over lace trim. Fold over top of TOP and find center. Match center of ribbon and lace and pin in place over TOP (Figure A). Work outward from middle and pin every 1/2 inch. On back of TOP, fold over top and pin ends of ribbon and lace to end of TOP. Work toward armhole and pin every 1/2 inch. The amount of excess lace and ribbon should be equal over each armhole. Top stitch lace, ribbon, and TOP folded edges.

3. Fold over bottom of SKIRT and top stitch.

4. Measure out 44 inches of double fold bias tape. Place bottom of TULLE SKIRT inside bias tape and top stitch.

5. Gather top of SKIRT and TULLE SKIRT until it is the length of the bottom of the TOP piece. With right sides of SKIRT and TULLE SKIRT facing TOP, pin in place about once every 1/2 inch. Sew a seam. Fold seam of SKIRT, TULLE SKIRT, and TOP up and top stitch along the bottom of the TOP piece.

6. Measure enough embroidered trim for length of bottom of TOP. Pin in place over bottom of TOP and top stitch along edges of embroidered trim.

7. With right sides together, sew seam from bottom of back of dress up to ──o point on pattern. Turn inside out. See pages 45-47 for a hook-and-loop tape *Closures* guide.

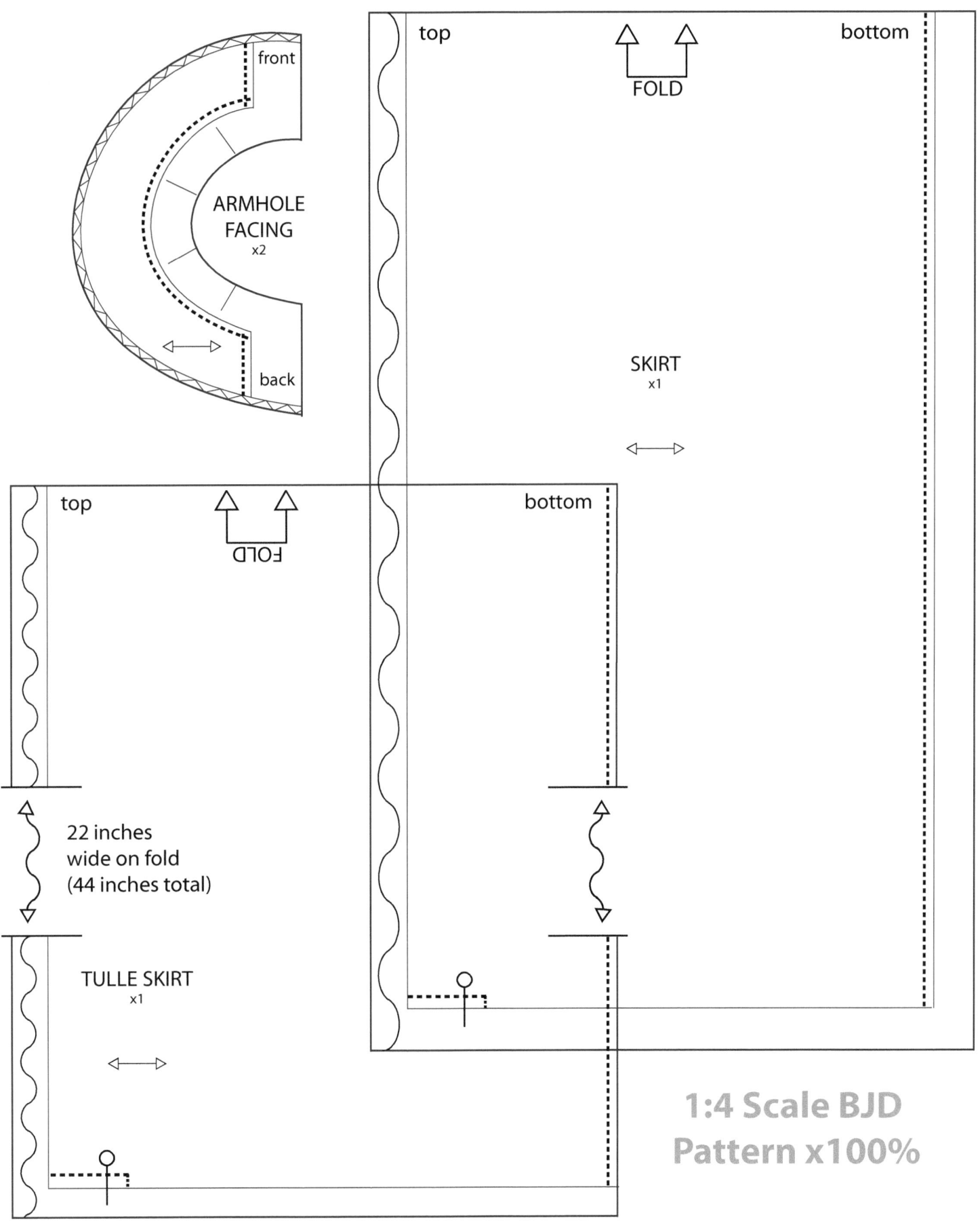

1:4 Scale Ball-Jointed Dolls

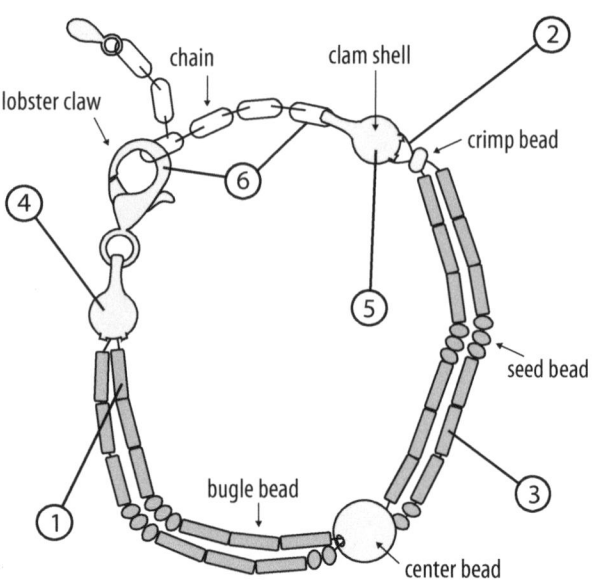

Hair Pin:

Photos on pages 20-22.

Supplies:
Small bobby pin
Glue gun
Thread
Ribbon (3 mm or less)
String of beads
Two feathers

Steps:
1. Tie two feathers together with thread.
2. Cut two pieces of ribbon in differing lengths. Tie together into a bow.
3. Using a generous amount of glue, hot glue feathers, string of beads, and bow onto bobby pin.

Necklace:

Photos on pages 20-22.

Supplies:
Lobster claw with chain
Jewelry wire
Two clam shells
Two crimp beads
Bugle beads
Seed beads
Center bead
Crimp pliers with cutter
Bead stopper

Steps:
Often, jewelry making kits are available at craft stores that have most of the items above included.

1. At the end of the jewelry wire, place a bead stopper (Figure A). Add desired string of beads for entire first row, making sure larger center bead is exactly in middle of the string of beads.
2. Once at end of row, make a 3-4 mm wide loop and place a crimp bead. Squeeze crimp bead with crimp pliers.
3. String second set of desired beads. Half way through string of beads, put jewelry wire through center bead, then finish string. The second row of beads should be slightly longer than first row with just a couple of seed beads.
4. Remove bead stopper and bring together both ends of string of beads. Place a crimp bead over both open ends of jewelry wire and squeeze with crimp pliers. Cut excess jewelry wire. Place crimp bead inside clam shell and gently squeeze with crimp pliers to hold in place.
5. At other end of string of beads, take loop made with jewelry wire and put through other clam shell. Gently squeeze clam shell closed with crimp pliers.
6. Add chain to one clam shell loop and lobster claw to other clam shell loop.

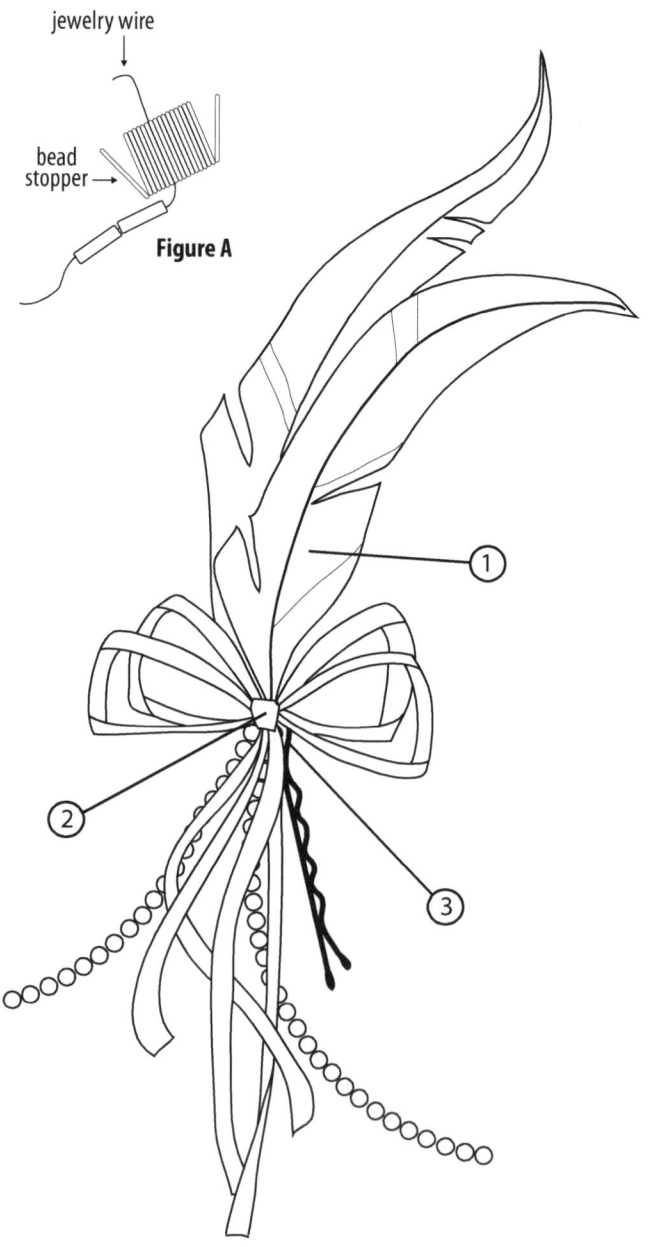

Chip

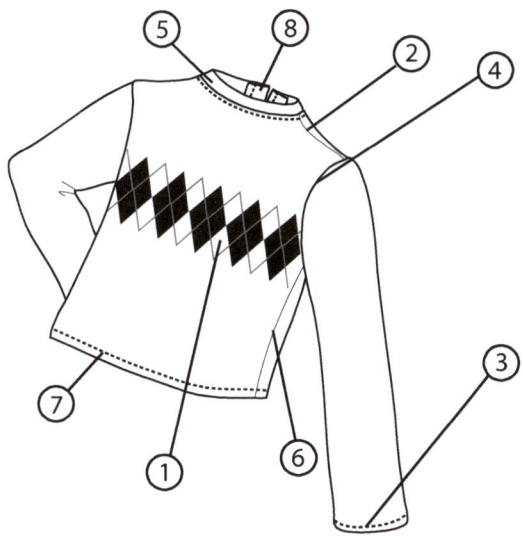

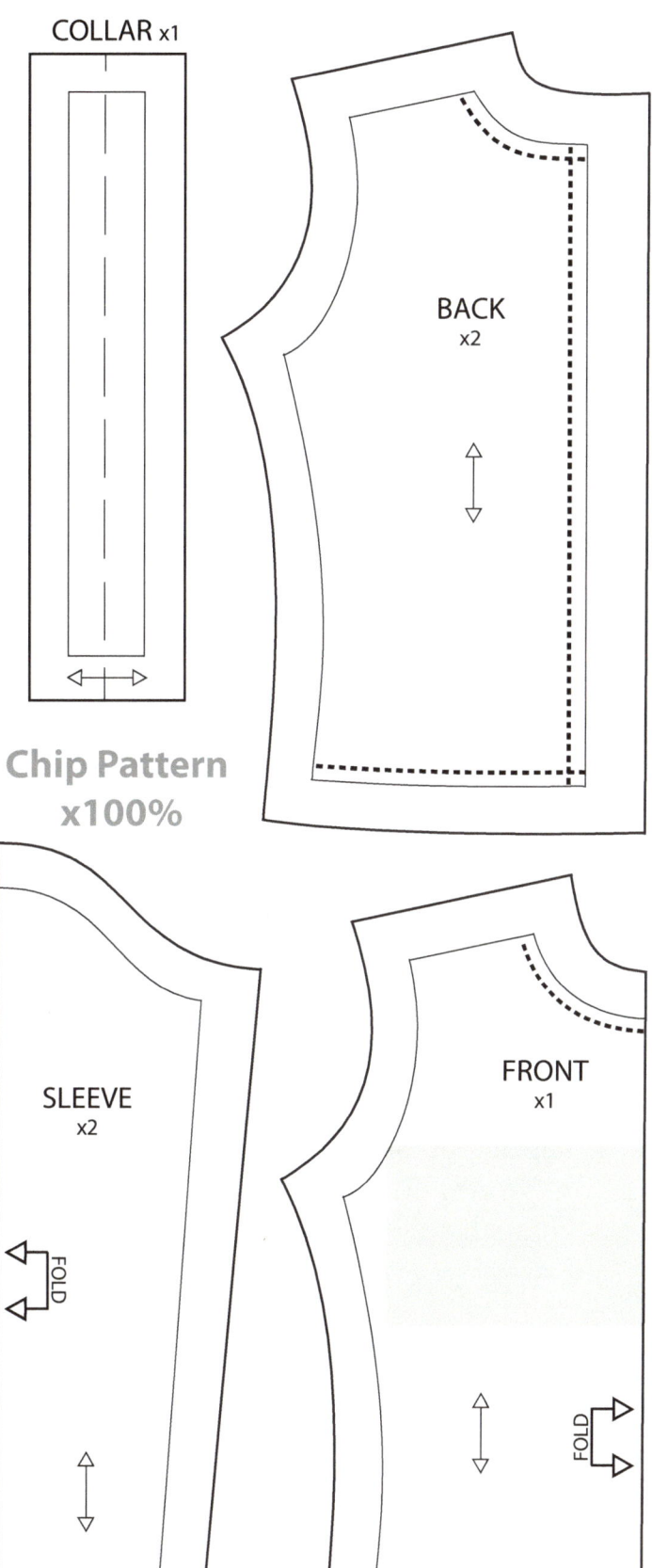

COLLAR x1

BACK x2

Chip Pattern x100%

SLEEVE x2

FRONT x1

Sweater:

Photo on pages 24-25.

Pattern Pieces:
FRONT x1, BACK x2, SLEEVE x2, and COLLAR x1

Supplies:
Sewing pattern basics (See pages 42-43)
Iron-on transfer paper (optional, see below)
Hook-and-loop closure tape

Steps:
Before following the steps outlined in the diagram, cut enough of each pattern piece for this sweater. A knit/stretchable fabric is recommended. If unable to find an argyle fabric, use an iron-on transfer to make argyle print.

1. If using an iron-on transfer for argyle print, apply to FRONT piece in gray shaded area on pattern.
2. Sew shoulder seams of FRONT to BACK pieces with the right sides together. Press seams open.
3. Fold bottom side of each SLEEVE over and top stitch.
4. Ease upper SLEEVE into each armhole using sewing pins or a basting stitch. Make sure right sides are together. Sew seam and repeat for other SLEEVE.
5. Fold COLLAR in half the long way, making sure to expose the right side of the fabric. With right sides together, sew seam of collar to neck opening. Fold COLLAR, FRONT, and BACK pieces down and top stitch over sweater (not collar).
6. With right sides together, sew seam from bottom of SLEEVE to armpit and then to the bottom of the garment. Clip curves, especially under armpit. Repeat on other side.
7. Fold over bottom of sweater and top stitch.
8. Fold over open edge of back pieces and sew hook-and-loop fastener into back of garment. See pages 45-47 for a helpful hook-and-loop *Closures* guide.

1:12 Scale Ball-Jointed Dolls

1:12 Scale BJD Pattern x100%

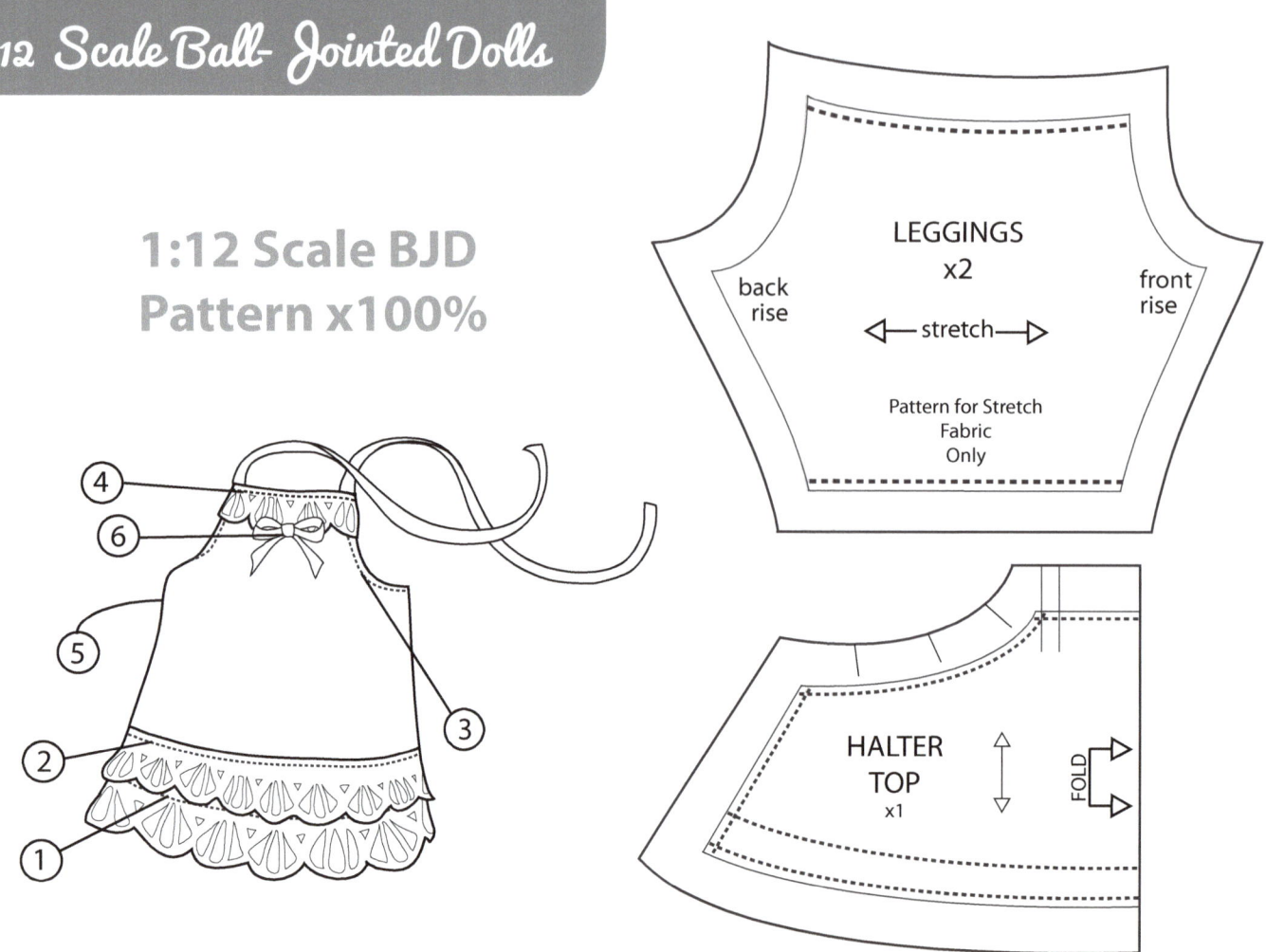

Halter Top:

Photos on pages 18-19.

Pattern Pieces:
HALTER TOP x1

Supplies:
Sewing pattern basics (See pages 42-43)
Lace trim
Ribbon (3 mm or smaller)
Hook-and-loop closure tape

Steps:
Before following the steps outlined in the diagram, cut enough of each pattern piece for this halter top.

1. Cut enough lace for the length of the bottom of the HALTER TOP. Fold over bottom of HALTER TOP and top stitch with lace pinned to the front of the fabric. Lace should be held in place with the top stitch.
2. Cut enough lace for the length of just above the previously top stitched lace. Top stitch the lace to the top of the HALTER TOP piece.
3. Fold over underarm areas and hold in place with pins or a basting stitch. Top stitch and repeat steps for other underarm area.
4. Cut enough lace for the length of the top front of the HALTER TOP. Cut 2 pieces of ribbon to be long enough to tie around the neck (at least 4 inches). Fold over the top front of HALTER TOP and pin lace to the front of the fabric. Pin ribbon at corners. Top stitch over ribbon, lace, and folded fabric. Lace and ribbon should be held in place with the top stitch.
5. Fold over open edge of back pieces and sew hook-and-loop closure into back of garment. See pages 45-47 for a helpful hook-and-loop *Closures* guide.
6. Tie a bow with ribbon and hand sew to front of HALTER TOP.

1:12 Scale Ball-Jointed Dolls

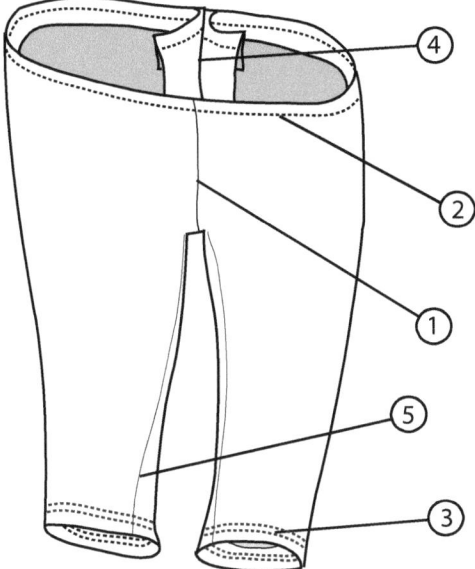

Leggings:

Photos on pages 18-19.

Pattern Pieces:
LEGGINGS x2

Supplies:
Sewing pattern basics (See pages 42-43)

Steps:
Before following the steps outlined in the diagram, cut enough of each pattern piece for these leggings. The pattern is specifically meant for stretch/knit fabric.

1. Sew seam of front rise of both LEGGINGS pieces with right sides together. If fabric is iron-friendly, press seams open.
2. Fold top of leggings over and top stitch.
3. Fold the bottom side of each pant leg over and top stitch with two rows of stitches.
4. Sew seam of back rise of both LEGGINGS pieces with right sides together.
5. With right sides together, sew seam from bottom of one pant leg up to the rise and then down the other pant leg. Turn inside out.

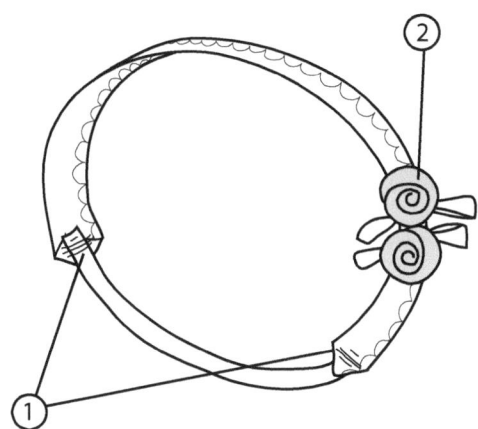

Head Band:

Photos on pages 18-19.

Supplies:
Needle and thread
Lace trim
Two ribbon roses
Elastic

Steps:
1. Measure out enough lace trim to go almost all the way around the head. Leave about 1 inch open for elastic. Fold corners of lace inward and hand sew about 1 inch of elastic to end of lace trim. Repeat with other end of lace and elastic.
2. Hand sew ribbon roses in desired areas of head band.

Photo Credits:

COVER: Normal skin Peak's Woods Fairy of Bugs (FOB) Lady Bee. DollGa Leeke World whisper blue wig. Acrylic eyes.

PAGE 2: Integrity Toys and Jason Wu Ye-Ye Collection Amelie. Barbie Basics Collection 1, Accessory Pack 1, sunglasses by Mattel. Shoes by PetWORKs. Earrings by MegannArt.

PAGE 3: Wake-Up momokoDOLL WUD012. Necklace by MegannArt. Wooden cuckoo clock ornament.

PAGE 4: Normal skin Peak's Woods Fairy of Bugs (FOB) Lady Bee. DollGa Leeke World whisper blue wig. Acrylic eyes. Backpack by Samantha Siakovich (anthrogirl on Den of Angels).

PAGE 5: Normal skin Peppermint Mint on Card exclusive doll by Asleep Eidolon. Wig by MegannArt. Chair by Greenbrier International, Inc. Bunny by Re-ment. Integrity Toys and Jason Wu red boots from Misaki, On the Go (Destination: Tokyo).

PAGE 6: CCS-momoko 12SS Home "Frosted Morning". Boots original with doll.

PAGES 6-7: momokoDOLL Skip to the Sunlight Through the Trees. Boots by SEKIGUCHI.

PAGES 8-9: Normal skin Peak's Woods Fairy of Bugs (FOB) Lady Bee. DollGa Leeke World dark cocoa wig. Acrylic eyes.

PAGES 10-11: Integrity Toys Dream Teen Poppy Parker. Earrings original with doll. Red shoes by SEKIGUCHI. Gold frame is a thrift store find. Miniature print of "Notre Dame" by Maximilien Luce (1899).

PAGES 12-13: Normal skin Peppermint Mint on Card exclusive doll by Asleep Eidolon. Wig and hair bow by MegannArt. Chair thrift store find. Bear is a "miniature doll house" find on eBay. Apple green shoes from ixtee Productions on eBay.

PAGES 14-15: momokoDOLL Beach Rodeo, slightly restyled hair by MegannArt. Bracelets original with Beach Rodeo. Slightly restyled hair by MegannArt. Bracelets original with doll.

PAGES 16-17: Integrity Toys OOAK Beatnik Blues Poppy Parker doll on loan from Alison Rasmussen. All jewelry by MegannArt. Table, blue dish, and wine glass by Re-ment. Frame is a thrift store find with heart artwork by MegannArt.

PAGES 18-19: Normal skin Peppermint Mint on Card exclusive doll by Asleep Eidolon. Wig and by MegannArt. Chair by Greenbrier International, Inc. Stuffed cat by MegannArt.

PAGES 20-23: Normal skin Peak's Woods Fairy of Bugs (FOB) Lady Bee. DollGa Leeke World dark cocoa wig. Acrylic eyes. Normal skin Peak's Woods Fairy of Bugs (FOB) Punky Beetle. Blond boy wig found on eBay.

PAGES 24-25: Integrity Toys My Generation Chip Farnsworth. Pants original with doll.

PAGE 25: Integrity Toys Dream Teen Poppy Parker dressed in clothing from patterns in this book. Earrings original with doll. Necklace by MegannArt.

PAGE 27: Odeco-can "Mermaid" of Odeco&Nikki. Boots by PetWORKs. Hand-painted watering can is a thrift store find.

PAGE 28: Rambra J-Doll by Groove Toys. Wooden cuckoo clock ornament. Cowboy boots by SEKIGUCHI.

PAGE 29: 2009 Tiny Betsy Basic Brunette by Tonner Doll Company. Shoes and socks by Tonner Doll Company, original with doll. Hair bow by MegannArt. Dog by Re-ment.

PAGE 30: Model Muse Barbie Basics Model No 06, Collection 001, by Mattel. Printed Cheshire Cat on tube top by MegannArt. Original Cheshire Cat illustration by John Tenniel. Purse and screen-printed fabric by MegannArt. Randall Craig shoes.

PAGE 31: Tan skin To You Mari by Limhwa Dolls. Wig by Ruby Red Galleria for Honee-B. Crown is a charm found on eBay.

PAGE 32: Barbie Fashionista Sporty Ken by Mattel (item model number V3397). Pants original with doll.

PAGE 33: Liv in Color! Sophie by Spin Master. Liv wig. Trinket and table are thrift store finds.

PAGE 34: 2009 Tiny Betsy Basic Brunette by Tonner Doll Company. Shoes and socks by Tonner Doll Company, original with doll. Lace skirt by MegannArt.

PAGE 35: Cornice Pullip by CheonSang Cheonha and Jun Planning.

PAGE 36: Tan skin To You Mari by Limhwa Dolls. Wig by Ruby Red Galleria for Honee-B. Basket and eggs by Re-ment.

PAGE 37: Model Muse Barbie Basics Model No 06, Collection 001, by Mattel. Earrings by MegannArt. Purse by Randall Craig.

PAGE 38: Liv in Color! Sophie by Spin Master. DollGa Leeke World dark cocoa wig. Fabric flowers are a thrift store find. Jewelry by MegannArt.

PAGE 49: Integrity Toys Dream Teen Poppy Parker dressed in clothing from pattern in this book. Earrings original with doll.

PAGE 54: CCS-momoko 12SS Home "Frosted Morning". Boots original with doll.

Suggested Resources:

Ball-Jointed Dolls for Beginners: Finding the Doll of Your Dreams by Alison Boyd Rasmussen, edited by Melissa Metheney

Steffie: Out of the Box (Complete Edition) by Alison Boyd Rasmussen

Alice: Out of the Box: A collection of Wonderland-themed dolls by Alison Boyd Rasmussen

Did you make a pattern from this book and want to share it? Go to dollybureau.com to find ways to post your work.

Interested in contributing to future editions of Dolly Bureau? Want an opportunity to promote your work? Send and email to info@dollybureau.com.

Patterns are for personal use only and may not be used in any form for profit.

www.ingramcontent.com/pod-product-compliance
Lightning Source LLC
Chambersburg PA
CBHW041529220426
43671CB00002B/26